AMERICA
IN THE
20TH
CENTURY

1920-1929

AMERICA IN THE 20TH CENTURY

SECOND EDITION
Revised and Expanded with Primary Sources

1920-1929

Janet McDonnell

MARSHALL CAVENDISH
NEW YORK • LONDON • TORONTO • SYDNEY

Marshall Cavendish
99 White Plains Road
Tarrytown, NY 10591

Website: www.marshallcavendish.com

© 1995, 2003 Marshall Cavendish Corporation

Library of Congress Cataloging-in-Publication Data

America in the 20th Century.-- 2nd ed., rev. and expanded with primary sources.
    p. cm.
    Includes bibliographical references and index.
    ISBN 0-7614-7364-5 (set)
    1. United States -- Civilization -- 20th century. I. Title: America in the twentieth century.
    E169.1.A471872   2003
    973.9--dc21

                                   2001052949

   ISBN 0-7614-7367-X (vol. 3)

Printed in Malaysia
Bound in the United States of America

06 05 04 03 02 5 4 3 2 1

Series created by Discovery Books

Series Editor: Paul Humphrey
Academic Consultants: Gregory Bush,
Chair of History Department, University of Miami, Coral Gables
Richard J. Taylor, History Department, University of Wisconsin, Parkside
Marshall Cavendish Editor: Peter Mavrikis
Marshall Cavendish Production Manager: Alan Tsai
Project Editors: Valerie Weber and Helen Dwyer
Picture Research: Gillian Humphrey
Design Concept: Laurie Shock
Designers: Ian Winton and Winsome Malcolm

(Frontispiece) Teaching old dogs new tricks. *This cover from* Life *magazine of 1926, by John Held, Jr., seems to capture the mood of the exuberant twenties.*

Contents

CHAPTER 1
Out of the War and into the Twenties

*November 7, 1918.
Jubilant crowd holds up
newspaper headlines pro-
claiming the end of World
War I. In fact, the press
was mistaken in reporting
the Armistice, which was
not signed until four days
later, when President
Wilson could announce to
Congress, "The war thus
comes to an end." The
fighting in Europe had left
around 115,000
Americans dead.*

The most popular nickname for the decade that spanned from 1920 to 1929 is The Jazz Age. For many people, it is a period that conjures up images of carefree flappers, smokey speakeasies, and stock market millionaires. It's been characterized as one long, Great Gatsby-style party of high living and wild antics. The truth, as always, is a lot more complicated than the popular myth. As

the twenties began, the United States was still unraveling itself from World War I. And as is always the case, peace did not come wrapped up in a neat, clean package, leaving the victors free to start celebrating. There were peace treaties to be written, economies to be rebuilt, and casualty lists to be read.

Although the United States was not eager to get involved in World

War I when the hostilities began in 1914, once it became involved in 1917, the country rallied around the cause. U.S. citizens bought Liberty bonds, built ships, rationed food, and sent two million of their boys to Europe to fight on foreign soil. Idealistic and eloquent, President Woodrow Wilson outlined the noble purpose of the war: "The world must be made safe for democracy."

When victory was announced on Armistice Day, November 11, 1918, the country rejoiced. Parade after parade of returning soldiers marched down Fifth Avenue in New York City through glittering flurries of ticker tape. Not only had the United States emerged victorious, but it emerged as the strongest military and economic power in the world. But the question that remained was whether or not Americans were ready to accept this new role. What most Americans wanted, now that the war was over, was a return to isolationism, to be left out of the political and economic turmoils of other nations. In reality, the American and European economies were tied together now more than ever before, and the United States had increasingly important security interests overseas.

As the country celebrated victory, expressions of pride took place beside demonstrations of hatred. Hastily stuffed effigies of the Kaiser, the leader of Germany during the war, were strung up on lampposts and burned to the cheers of gathered crowds. Americans were still filled with the fighting spirit. Yet they were also eager to begin a new era of peace, to put aside public duty, and to get back to their own individual concerns.

But settling that peace was proving

Woodrow Wilson hoped to rally support for the League of Nations and thus make the world "safe for democracy." His ill health and opposition in the Congress thwarted those plans.

extremely difficult. President Wilson had almost killed himself trying. He was determined that World War I would not have been fought in vain but would produce a better world than existed before the war. In December of 1918, Wilson sailed for the peace conference in France believing that it was the United States' "fortunate duty to assist by example, by sober, friendly counsel, and by material aid in the establishment of just democracy throughout the world." But, in Versailles, he discovered that the Allies, while in a sober mood, were not in a friendly one. They had suffered far greater casualties and damage to their countries than the United States had, and now their goal seemed to be vengeance against Germany. Although they were receptive to Wilson's plan for a League of Nations, they wanted guarantees that the United States would come to the defense of the other nations in the

"Here was the new generation...dedicated more than the last to the fear of poverty and the worship of success; grown up to find all gods dead, all wars fought, all faiths in man shaken."

F. Scott Fitzgerald, *This Side of Paradise*

> *"Too many people have free speech in this country."*
>
> A. Mitchell Palmer, U.S. Attorney General

league. Wilson was forced to return home with a very different treaty than the one he had sought. Though in his idealistic heart he could not possibly have been confident in the justice of the treaty, Wilson pursued Congress' ratification with uncompromising zeal.

The extreme isolationists in the Senate wanted nothing to do with the league. Others wanted to amend the treaty. Wilson was unwilling to change a word. Opposed by Congress, Wilson took his message to the people. During an exhausting speaking tour in the summer of 1919, which took the president by train to city after city for speech after eloquent speech, Wilson collapsed with a nervous breakdown, made worse by a recent bout of influenza. A week later he had a cerebral hemorrhage that paralyzed his left side and nearly killed him. As the new decade opened, Wilson was an invalid in the White House, still committed to getting the treaty ratified in its unchanged form though it was destined to fail. For the remaining year and a half of his term, Wilson saw almost nobody. Those wishing to communicate with the president, even on important government business, had to do so by letter. The letters were not always answered, and a rumor spread that it was Mrs. Wilson who was running the government. Whether this is true or not, Wilson's physical condition did result in a lack of direction in domestic policy that proved disastrous for civil liberties and overall demobilization.

The hundreds of thousands of men returning from the war were not nearly as concerned with who ran the White House as they were with the more immediate problems they faced. Though the twenties are known as a time of prosperity, the country that these men returned to in 1919 and 1920 was in a recession. With the end of the war came a drop in government spending and a weakening of the export market. Business bankruptcies tripled from 1919 to 1920. Wages were cut and workers laid off. On top of the unemployment problem, everyone was complaining about the high cost of living. Housing costs were especially high, due in large part to a serious housing shortage. Some who could find neither a job nor affordable housing built shanty towns. One thing was painfully clear: the end of the war did not by any means bring an end to the United States' problems at home.

The Strangers Among Us

In fact, the war added fuel to the fire of one problem. The patriotic spirit that united the country in purpose during the war also led to a chauvinistic nationalism that made many Americans suspicious of the "foreigners" among them. Of course, the United States is a nation of foreigners. Except for American Indians (most of whom were confined to reservations by this time), everyone came to the United States from foreign shores. But to the Americans who wrapped themselves in the red, white, and blue, the newly arrived immigrants, naturalized or not, were foreigners and therefore suspicious. The newly formed American Legion announced that among its goals was "100 percent Americanism." The Citizens' Protective League, the American Defense Society, the National Security League and the National Civic League pursued similar goals. Under the supervision of the reformers of earlier decades, Americanization had done much to help the immigrants in U.S. cities. But in the

BOLSHEVISM

REDS

ANARCHY

This 1919 cartoon shows a Bolshevik creeping under the U.S. flag. Communist revolution in Russia and a wave of strikes in the coal, steel, construction, and railroad industries ushered in the "Red Scare." The journalist Walter Lippmann wrote at the time, "The people... are far more afraid of Lenin than they ever were of the Kaiser."

hands of superpatriots, it could, and did, lead to such bullying behavior as forcing immigrants to kiss the flag.

The worst suspicion that a foreigner could fall under was that he or she was a Bolshevik, or Communist. As 1919 turned into 1920, the big Red Scare was in full bloom in America. The Bolshevik Revolution, which turned Russia into the world's first Communist country in November 1917, seemed likely to spread to other countries in eastern and central Europe. When the Russian Communists announced that they were dedicated to transplanting the revolution to other countries, the question arose: Could the United States be at risk? A small group of radicals with attention-grabbing bombs convinced many Americans that the answer was yes.

In April of 1919, thirty-six bombs were sent through the mail to political and business leaders around the country. All but one were intercepted before they could cause serious injury, but the blazing headlines that spread the news of the bombs terrified most Americans. On June 2 that same year, the home of Attorney General A. Mitchell Palmer was one of several bomb targets. Palmer was uninjured in the attack, but the bomb had its effect.

It set Palmer off on an "anti-radical campaign" that escalated the Red Scare to a level of irrational hysteria and violated scores of civil liberties in the process.

During the war, political repression and censorship were considered a necessary part of the war effort, and the good patriot did not complain. When those methods were continued after the war in the name of protecting the United States from Bolshevism, Americans for the most part again accepted it. On the second day of the new decade, the Justice Department conducted massive raids of "radical" gatherings at bakeries, meeting halls, and restaurants around the country.

September 1919. Massachusetts governor Calvin Coolidge with the militiamen he had ordered into Boston to help break the police strike. Soon after the striking officers had been fired, gangs freely walked the city, committing acts of vandalism, looting stores and assaulting passers by. The violence only subsided after the National Guard was brought in to restore order.

Nearly two thousand people were arrested, most of them without a warrant and for dubious reasons.

Labor Loses Ground

Organized labor was also hurt by people who were allegedly trying to save the United States. During the war, labor's position had improved. The progressive Wilson administration felt it could not afford labor unrest that would halt production, especially of munitions. To insure labor's cooperation, the government created the War Labor Board and encouraged collective bargaining (negotiations between representatives of the workers and their employer). The moderate labor movement gained power, importance, and hope that the improvements would continue. However, the more radical elements of the labor movement, like the Industrial Workers of the World (IWW), suffered as the government set up its own unions to counter radical demands.

But by the spring of 1919, the wartime system of arbitration was dismantled, and business was determined to push back the advances made by labor. Unions were depicted as anti-American, perhaps even part of a Bolshevik plot to overthrow capitalism. Workers were forced to sign "yellow dog contracts," which were a promise not to join unions. Courts around the country ordered injunctions against labor meetings. Wilson, in ill health and distracted by the league, was no help.

Faced with inflationary prices and low wages, labor turned to its strongest weapon, the strike. The year 1919 was the most strike-ridden year in America's history. On September 9, the underpaid Boston police did the unthinkable — they struck for higher wages. The governor of Massachusetts, Calvin Coolidge, refused to negotiate, writing "There can be no right to strike against the public safety by anybody, anywhere, anytime." It was a statement that won him instant popularity around the nation and would lead to his vice presidential nomination in the 1920 election. The Boston strike lasted two days. Every striking policeman was fired.

A huge steel strike, begun in the same month, also ended without any gains for the strikers. As the twenties began, labor had tasted defeat but was still hungry for change.

Wartime Legacy: Prohibition and Women's Suffrage

The most popular topic of conversation on the eve of the twenties was not, however, the labor strikes. It was the approaching prohibition, the ban against the manufacture and sale of alcohol. The Eighteenth Amendment was set to take effect on January 16, 1920.

For years, the prohibition movement had been making steady headway. Since at least the turn of the century, reformers had been denouncing alcohol as a danger to society as well as to the human body. During the war, the idea of prohibition became patriotic, a way to keep the nation strong — for a drunk worker is not a productive worker. By 1919, many states were already dry, or had prohibited the sale of alcohol. (At least they had laws that said they did.) Although the Eighteenth Amendment had popular support, the prospect of becoming a dry nation had many people in a decidedly nervous mood. Still, while

"Yes, sir; the girls work 10 hours a day, and then on Saturday you cannot eat a bite of lunch from the time you get in the plant until you get out Saturday, and when you think about working until 11:30 through the week and getting a lunch at 11:30 and then have to work until 1 o'clock on Saturday before you get anything to eat, you are exhausted."

Margaret Bowen, Elizabethton, Tennessee, textile worker

there was time, they could build up their supplies and prepare for the coming dry spell. But the country was to find that while passing prohibition was relatively simple, its effects would be quite complicated.

There was yet another change scheduled to take effect at the start of the next decade. In 1920, women would for the first time take part in electing the president of the United States. The American suffragettes had worked long and hard for the right to vote, and in June of 1919, the Nineteenth Amendment was ratified, finally guaranteeing women this most basic civil right. The twenties would bring many changes to women's lives. Some of those changes were ones that the feminists of 1919 would have neither predicted nor desired.

Of course, what makes the beginning of a new decade so exciting is that it is sure to bring changes that no one would have predicted. Who would have guessed, for example, that radio, which in 1919 was only interesting to a few science-minded hobbyists, would soon be entertaining the nation? Or that instead of watching ticker tape parades, Americans would become obsessed with watching the ticker tape itself to find out how the stock market was doing? The trend against strict Victorian/Puritan morals and manners that began before the war was taken up again with renewed energy in the twenties. It was anyone's guess where this rebellion would lead.

The dawn of the twenties found a nation that was worn out from war and disillusioned by peace. Americans were restless and, as always, hopeful that the future would bring solutions and better times. They were about to begin an exciting era known as The Jazz Age.

After more than seventy years of struggle, women could at last participate in the democratic process at the national level. The Nineteenth Amendment did not give women equal rights with men, however. In many states women were not allowed to serve on juries, hold public office, enter into business, or sign contracts without their husbands' consent.

CHAPTER 2
A Time of Intolerance

The Red Scare

By January of 1920, the United States was virtually paralyzed by the grip of the great Red Scare. Suspicion had spread to every corner of the country fueled by claims that public schools, universities, churches, the press, Congress, and even the president's cabinet had been infiltrated by Bolsheviks.

Teachers who sought to shine the light of knowledge on the situation in Russia by studying Bolshevik doctrines with their students risked losing their jobs. Ministers who expressed sympathy for the goals of organized

A 1921 cartoon entitled Coming Out of the Smoke. *Steelworkers, who had organized the first modern strike involving a whole industry, had just one demand — that they be allowed one day's rest each week. At that time, they worked twelve hours a day, seven days a week. However, the steel companies, aided and abetted by sympathetic press, termed the strike a radical uprising and thus alienated public opinion from the strikers.*

(Right) Isadora Duncan, the American dancer and supporter of Bolshevism, was booed off stage on October 24, 1922 after declaring her political beliefs. At the time she was married to a Russian poet and had started a dance school in Moscow in a house given to her by the Soviet leader, Lenin.

labor were criticized as leaning toward Bolshevism. Journals that spoke out against such a witch hunt mentality were labeled radical, and the average man on the street thought twice before subscribing to certain magazines for fear of the suspicion they would arouse in his neighbors or colleagues.

During this period, people who expressed liberal democratic ideas were lumped together with those calling for a violent revolution. Openly criticizing the government or capitalism could land a person in jail. Membership in the wrong group could lead to calls for deportation. Though freedom of speech was still protected under the Constitution, it was a risky business to exercise it.

How could a democratic nation founded on the principle of civil liberties come to this point? What could make Americans so fearful of a Bolshevik under every bed that they would ignore the violation of civil rights? Actually, several different factors combined to kindle the Red Scare. Once ignited, the sparks were fanned into a raging fire.

The Radical Movement

The irrational hysteria that gripped the nation was not, of course, created out of thin air. Vladimir Ilich Lenin and Leon Trotsky shocked the world with the Russian Revolution in November 1917. To Americans who were seeking a return to normal, peaceful living after the war, the Bolsheviks' call for a worldwide revolution was not part of the plan. The Communist goal to abolish all private property was downright un-American, and their slogan, "Workers

of the World unite, you have nothing to lose but your chains" sent a chill down many an American businessman's back.

There were, however, some Americans who cheered on the Bolsheviks. In the fall of 1919, two Communist parties were born in the United States, and they did indeed seek to spread the revolution. The Communist party and the Communist Labor party were created from the left wing — the more liberal or radical branch — of the Socialist party. Prior to World War I, the Socialists had enough of a following to win many seats in local and state governments. But when the leaders of the party spoke out against the war, Socialists were viewed as pro-German and unpatriotic. Many of their leaders were jailed, and soon Socialists began quarreling among themselves over the issue of communism. The left wing of the party was dominated by foreign-born members. These working-class immigrants, without a firm grasp of the principles upon which the nation was founded, believed Bolshevism could succeed in the United States. Their principles were spelled out in their manifesto: "The world is in crisis. Capitalism, the prevailing system of society is in process of disintegration and collapse. . . . Humanity can be saved from its last excesses only by the Communist Revolution."

Another group that cheered on the Bolsheviks was the Industrial Workers of the World (IWW), or Wobblies, as they were called. A radical labor union, the Wobblies were not only antiwar, but had in the past professed a belief in violence to achieve their goals. Already known for their inflammatory slogans, the Wobblies quickly took up the Bolshevik line, with lyrics such as these:

All hail to the Bolsheviki!
We will fight for our class and
be free
A Kaiser, King, or Czar, no
matter which you are
You're nothing of interest to me;
If you don't like the red flag of
Russia
If you don't like the spirit so true,
Then just be like the cur in the
story
And lick the hand that's
robbing you.

The average American worker was skeptical of the Wobblies, and their membership was relatively low. Still, the Wobblies had a way of drawing a great deal of attention and fear. In 1919, the Wobblies organized a general strike in Seattle that shut down the city for two days. Though the strike was defeated and the workers' demands were not answered, the incident left many Americans wondering, "Is this how the revolution will start?" As strike after bitter strike broke out in 1919, the suspicion increased that the Bolsheviks were behind it all.

Just how widespread was the Communist influence in the United States? In 1919, both Communist parties combined had seventy thousand members, equal to one tenth of 1 percent of the population. Why so much fear over such a small segment of the populace? Though their numbers were small, their voices were loud. The Communists distributed many radical journals and leaflets, filled with Marxist propaganda, including Lenin's letter "To the American Workers." And in addition to the Communist party members, there were an uncounted number of so-called parlor reds. These were the sophisticated, often wealthy intellectuals who usually supported the Bolshevik cause with more words than action. For many of them, communism was of interest as a passing fad rather than as a passionate cause. Even so, frightened Americans pointed to the parlor reds as a sign of just how far the hateful, radical Bolshevism had spread.

Even more frightening than the propaganda and the parlor reds were the bombs. Of the thirty-six mail bombs mentioned earlier, the first was delivered to Mayor Ole Hanson of Seattle. Uninjured by the bomb, Hanson wrote a book and embarked on a speaking tour of the nation,

"We must bring home to the people the truth that a compromise with Bolshevism is to barter away our inheritance."

Lee Overman,
United States senator,
North Carolina

Eugene V. Debs in prison clothes in 1920. Socialist leader and presidential candidate since 1900, Debs was sent to prison for ten years in 1918 when he defended the radical Industrial Workers of the World, the Bolshevik Revolution in Russia, and pacifism. He was pardoned by President Harding and released from prison on Christmas Eve, 1921. He once said, "I am for socialism because I am for humanity."

describing how he beat the Bolshevik strike in his city. He was just one example of the many people who profited from the proliferation of the Red Scare.

Spreading the Fear

Undoubtedly some of the people who proclaimed that the country was in danger of a radical revolution really believed it to be true. But for many others, the Bolshevik label was a handy weapon to use against any and all enemies, including liberal reformers, organized labor, or anyone else who rubbed someone the wrong way.

During the war, independent agencies were formed to bolster patriotism and in general help the war effort. With names like the American Protective League, these groups turned their attention to Bolshevik bashing after the war. Soon their goals changed from promoting patriotism to strengthening conservatism. Funded

mainly by corporations and businessmen, these superpatriots circulated lists of "radical" journals to be boycotted and published essays with titles such as "If Bolshevism Came to America." The Americans who had been conditioned during the war to hate the enemy quickly transferred that emotion from the Germans to the Bolsheviks.

Another main proponent of the Red Scare was Attorney General A. Mitchell Palmer. Ironically, Palmer was raised a Quaker and had a reputation as a reformer himself. He even appealed to Wilson to release the jailed Socialist leader Eugene V. Debs, to no avail. When the thirty-six mail bombs were discovered, the public clamored for action against the radicals. Palmer refused to panic. But when his own home was the target of a bomb just over one month later, the attorney general had a change of heart. Soon after, Palmer requested and received $500,000 from Congress to fund an antiradical campaign. Thus began what would later be called "Palmer's Reign of Terror."

With Wilson an invalid in the White House, Palmer ran the Justice Department virtually unchecked. He hired a young J. Edgar Hoover to head the General Intelligence Division, a new department created to "root out the radicals." Among the so-called radicals that were rooted out were Charlie Chaplin and Will Rogers. Palmer compared communism in the United States to a prairie fire "sweeping over every American institution of law and order."

Two of Palmer's most powerful weapons were raids and deportations. To conduct the raids more easily, arrest warrants were considered optional. Deportations were decided without a trial, since it was "not considered a punishment." On December 21, 1919, 249 alien radicals were deported. The press, which also played a role in heightening the hysteria, quickly dubbed the ship carrying the deportees the "Soviet Ark." Palmer promised that many more Soviet Arks would follow. Four hundred of the suspected radicals who

TORCH OF FREEDOM

SOCIALISM

For further information see primary source entries on pages

11: 1481–82, 1502–04

An early poster for the Industrial Workers of the World (IWW). With the success of the Bolshevik revolution in Russia, IWW leaders redoubled their efforts to secure better working conditions and higher wages for their members and to overthrow their bosses. Not all American labor organizations were as radical. The American Federation of Labor (the AFL) denounced Bolshevism, and leader Samuel Gompers even tried to have members with Bolshevik sympathies expelled from the union.

Outside the IWW headquarters, members of the radical union are lined up and searched by police in 1920 during Attorney General Palmer's "Reign of Terror."

were rounded up in the raids of January 2, 1920 were sent to a prison on Deer Island, where conditions were miserable. One man went crazy, one committed suicide, and two died of pneumonia.

Unaware or unconcerned about such violations of civil liberties, the American public hailed Palmer as a hero. This suited him just fine, as Palmer had his eye on the White House. He hoped to ride the Red Scare all the way into the 1920 elections. As fortune would have it, however, he wouldn't quite make it.

The Fading of the Red Scare

By the time the primaries were underway, the hysteria of the Red Scare had calmed down, and by election time in the fall of 1920, most Americans were tired of hearing about Bolsheviks. Looking back, we can find a number of causes for the fading of the Red Scare. For one thing, the Communist threat did not seem as great as it once had. It seemed clear by this time that France, Italy, and Germany would not fall victim to the spreading Communist menace. And in the United States, the threat also seemed weaker since many radicals began to think it wise to keep their opinions to themselves. In general, the fighting spirit that had persisted after the war was finally giving way to a more peaceful mood in the country. Americans were turning their attention to the new affordable cars, changing hemlines, and exciting events in sports. Newspapers began giving more space to advertisements and articles about the latest fads and less space to exaggerated stories about wild-eyed radicals.

Alongside these subtle developments, some specific events occurred that made Americans stop and wonder if the Red Scare wasn't getting a bit out of hand. When the New York legislature voted to expel five Socialist members simply for being Socialists, people began to wonder, "Where will this all end?" Politicians and journalists around the country decried this threat to representative government. Many people finally realized that the more immediate danger to the principles and institutions of democracy, such as free speech, came not from alien radicals but from Red Scare zealots. Supreme Court Justice Oliver Wendell Holmes, Jr. spoke out against a proposed peacetime sedition law by comparing radical opinions to champagne: "The quickest way to let them get flat is to let them get exposed to air."

Reasoned minds prevailed in other areas too. In March of 1920, Louis F. Post became acting secretary of labor when the previous sec-

retary fell ill. The Labor Department had been issuing thousands of warrants to the Justice Department to use in their mass raids. Post canceled two thousand warrants and released almost half of the people rounded up in the January raids. When the House sought to impeach Post for "coddling the Reds," Post turned the tables by exposing how the Justice Department had been misusing the deportation laws.

Palmer made one last effort to revive the Red Scare. He predicted that May Day, 1920, was the date for the Communist revolution in the United States. All around the country, cities beefed up security and braced themselves for the attack. Nothing happened. Though Palmer claimed that the country had prevented the revolution by being prepared, Americans weren't buying it.

Ironically, just as Americans were calming down, an event occurred to test their nerves. On

In September 1920, a massive explosion ripped through Wall Street, New York City, the business center of the nation. Despite the loss of life and casualties, the bomb attack did not have the impact it might have had a year earlier, when the Red Scare was at its height. As the Cleveland Plain Dealer *of September 18, 1920, put it, "The public is merely shocked, not terrorized, much less converted to the merits of anarchism. Business and life as usual...functioning as if nothing had happened."*

September 16, 1920, a huge bomb exploded on the corner of Broad and Wall Streets in New York City, the heart of American capitalism. The blast was so powerful that people standing near sixth floor windows were badly burned. Thirty-four people were killed and over two hundred injured. The identities of those who planted the bomb were never discovered. Nevertheless, had the incident occured one year earlier, it would have left many Americans wondering whether it was a Bolshevik plot to overthrow the government. Instead, Americans were horrified, but not terrorized. The Red Scare had died down. But, like the Wall Street bombing, it would leave many scars behind.

Anti-immigrant Feelings

One lingering effect of the Red Scare and the war was a fear of foreigners. Even after the scare died down, the superpatriots continued their crusade for "100 percent Americanism." In addition to their demands for the "Americanization" of school texts and loyalty oaths for teachers, they called for stricter immigration laws. General Leonard Wood expressed what many were feeling when he said, "We do not want to be a dumping ground for radicals, agitators, reds, who do not understand our ideals."

Especially suspect were southern and eastern Europeans, who made up about 80 percent of the immigrants by World War I. Unlike the northern Europeans who came earlier and helped settle the West, these new arrivals were mainly Catholics and Jews with unfamiliar customs. They were often uneducated and had little experience with democratic society. As such, they were not as easily assimilated into American life. In addition, most of the new immigrants stayed in the large cities, especially on the East Coast, forming enclaves that made assimilation less necessary.

In 1921, the United States instituted an annual immigration quota for the first time. It limited immigration to 3 percent of the number of each nationality present according to the 1910 census, with a maximum quota of 357,000. The 1924

This diagram shows the changing mix of immigrants between 1910 and 1930.

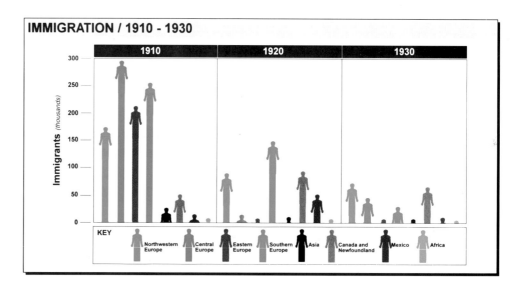

Immigration Act cut that number to less than half. More importantly, it discriminated against eastern and southern Europeans seeking entry into the United States by limiting annual immigration to 2 percent of the 1890 census, when far fewer of the new immigrants were present. The 1924 act excluded Asians altogether, which greatly angered the Japanese government. But in response to the possible threat of resignation by the Japanese Ambassador, one senator remarked, "East is East and West is West....Japan will recognize the full wisdom of our choice."

In truth, the nation had good reasons for putting restrictions on immigration. Since the turn of the century, over fourteen and a half million immigrants had poured into the country. Projections indicated that the flow would continue at the rate of at least one million per year if not restricted. The United States simply could not absorb so many people, especially with unemployment still high. But aside from such

Newly arrived immigrants undergo a health examination at New York's Ellis Island in 1920 before being allowed into the country.

> *"These immigrants adopt the language of the native American, they wear his clothes, they steal his name and they are beginning to take his women, but they seldom adopt his religion or understand his ideals."*
>
> Madison Grant,
> *The Passing of the Great Race*

practical considerations, an anti-immigrant prejudice permeated the country. The large influx of foreigners worried many Americans. Studies appeared claiming the intellectual superiority of the Nordic groups over other ethnic and racial groups.

Perhaps the best example of the anti-foreigner mood in the country is the Sacco and Vanzetti case. In April of 1920, a paymaster and a guard were murdered during a payroll robbery. Two weeks later, police arrested Nicola Sacco and Bartolomeo Vanzetti and charged them with the crime. Sacco and Vanzetti were Italian aliens and professed anarchists. Their trial included flimsy evidence, questionable eyewitnesses, and an apparently prejudiced judge. They were convicted and sentenced to death.

The execution was postponed repeatedly as protests broke out across the United States and abroad. The case became a unifying public cause for intellectuals including poet Edna St. Vincent Millay, writer John Dos Passos, and scientist Albert Einstein. Some were sympathetic to the political views of the two anarchists, while others were simply outraged by what appeared to be a frame-up. Americans on the whole were divided in their opinions of the guilt or innocence of Sacco and Vanzetti. Meanwhile, the two Italians spent six years in prison. In 1925, after another Italian prisoner confessed to the crime, the defense requested a new trial. The motion was denied, and the execution date was set.

On August 23, 1927, Sacco and Vanzetti were executed by electric

Nicola Sacco and Bartolomeo Vanzetti (front, center) are led hand-cuffed to court, charged with the April 1920 murder of a paymaster and a guard. Their arrest, trial, and subsequent execution were seen by many as blatantly unjust.

chair. Protesters tried to storm the prison but found that it was heavily guarded. In other parts of the world, American embassies were stoned and American flags were defaced. The case is still debated to this day, but most would agree that the anti-foreigner attitude in the United States played a part in the deaths of Sacco and Vanzetti.

Racial Tensions

Intolerance took another shape as well, in the form of racism. In the summer of 1919, bloody race riots broke out across the country in cities such as Washington, D.C., and Chicago, where nearly forty people were killed and over five hundred injured during a week of violence. One major cause for the tensions was the massive wartime migration of blacks that continued into the twenties, as did the riots.

During and after World War I, hundreds of thousands of African-Americans travelled north in the hopes of finding a better life. They were lured by the prospect of better jobs, the urging of the northern black press, and a desire to escape the miserable conditions in the south. In New York, the black population increased from around 150,000 in 1920 to over 300,000 in 1930. Other northern cities experienced similar increases. The result was overcrowded ghettoes. Though the newly arrived African-Americans found better jobs than those in the South, they were still low paying, unskilled positions. The poor whites in the cities resented the black competition for jobs, and it was in that segment of society that the most virulent racism was to be found.

When the tensions erupted in violence, many whites felt that African-Americans needed to be "put back in their place." A *New York Times* editorial about the riots pointed out that before the war, most blacks were "well-behaved" and "admitted the superiority of the white race." After the war, African-American soldiers who had fought for their country (even though in segregated units)

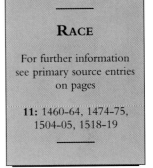

RACE

For further information see primary source entries on pages

11: 1460-64, 1474-75, 1504-05, 1518-19

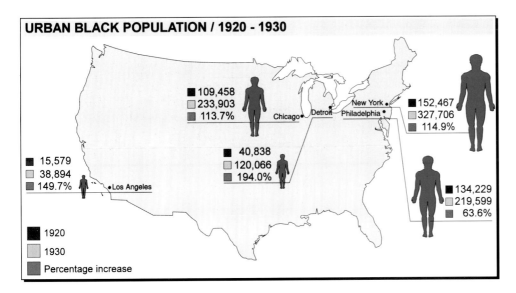

URBAN BLACK POPULATION / 1920 - 1930

- 109,458
- 233,903
- 113.7%
- Chicago

- 152,467
- 327,706
- 114.9%
- New York, Detroit, Philadelphia

- 15,579
- 38,894
- 149.7%
- Los Angeles

- 40,838
- 120,066
- 194.0%

- 134,229
- 219,599
- 63.6%

- 1920
- 1930
- Percentage increase

This map shows the growth of the urban black population during the 1920s.

naturally returned home believing that their military service would earn them a better position in society. But white society was not so willing to accept a change in the social order. Red Scare tactics were even used to suppress African-Americans, with

Marcus Garvey. (1887-1940)

As the controversial leader of one of the most powerful black movements in the history of the United States, Marcus Garvey won many followers as well as enemies among black Americans in the twenties. Born in Jamaica, Garvey came to the United States in 1916 to raise money for his newly created Universal Negro Improvement Association. Garvey founded the UNIA upon three basic principles: he believed that harmony would come through racial and ethnic separatism; he advocated universal solidarity of all black people; and he protested against colonialism, calling for a return to "Africa for the Africans."

In the early twenties, the UNIA was in its prime with nearly one million members in forty countries. Interest was especially strong in the United States. To American blacks who felt shut out of democracy, Marcus Garvey was a vision of hope as he stood in his uniform and white-plumed hat crying, "Up! Up, you mighty race!"

Garvey believed it was essential to establish black institutions to set up a base of black power and build a framework for a future "Negro nation." In all of the major U.S. cities, the UNIA launched business, social, and religious organizations. The spirit of black pride and independence engendered by the UNIA drew in thousands of American blacks.

However, civil rights organizations such as the NAACP, which had been steadily working towards integration for decades, were deeply at odds with the UNIA. Not only was Garvey's zealous call for black separatism directly contrary to their goals, but the growth of the UNIA threatened to undermine the power of competing black organizations.

The downfall of the UNIA began in 1922. The southern chapters were being harassed by the Ku Klux Klan, and Garvey decided to respond. He went to Atlanta to meet with a Klan leader, hoping that by explaining that they both had the common goal of racial separatism, the harassment would end. When word of the meeting leaked out, Garvey was attacked from both within and outside the UNIA, and bitter divisions threatened to destroy his movement.

In 1923, Garvey and three officers of the Black Star Line, a failed shipping business launched by UNIA, were tried for mail fraud. The main piece of evidence in the questionable trial was an empty envelope from the Black Star Line. The judge, a member of the NAACP, gave Garvey the maximum sentence, five years. Coolidge ordered his release after two years. Though Garvey died penniless and almost forgotten in 1940, many of his beliefs were carried on by later black leaders including Malcolm X.

blazing headlines such as: "REDS TRY TO STIR NEGROES TO REVOLT."

But despite scare tactics and intimidation, African-Americans were determined to move forward, not backward. Their struggles for a better life included many different strategies. A black leader from Jamaica named Marcus Garvey preached black separatism, while the National Association for the Advancement of Colored

People pushed for integration. Mary McCleod Bethune, a courageous black educator, brought quality schools and higher education to southern blacks. During the twenties, it became apparent that black Americans were increasingly ready to stand up for their rights.

The Rise of the Ku Klux Klan

Amid this atmosphere of intolerance, suspicion, and social restlessness, the Ku Klux Klan was reborn. Inactive since the 1870s, the KKK was revived by Imperial Wizard William J. Simmons in 1915 with an ad announcing "The World's Greatest Secret, Social, Patriotic, Fraternal, Beneficiary Order." Though the Klan was somewhat slow in getting started up again, during the

twenties its membership exploded.

The superpatriots' crusade for 100 percent Americanism paved the way for the rise of the KKK. The Klan claimed to speak for the "old stock" Americans, meaning the Americans descended from the Nordic pioneers, whom they believed to be the superior race. To be for the white race, they preached, was to be against all others, including blacks, Jews, Asians, Catholics, and foreigners. In their theory, a "mongrelized civilization," which the United States was quickly becoming, was doomed to fail. As Hiram Wesley Evans, the new Imperial Wizard, explained: "First in the Klansman's mind is patriotism — America for Americans. He believes religiously that a betrayal of Americanism or the American race is treason to the most sacred of trusts, a trust from his fathers and a trust from God. He

Mounted policemen escort a wounded African-American to a zone of safety during the Chicago race riots of 1919. Whites had been trying to drive the black residents out of their homes because they felt themselves and their jobs threatened by the many thousands of African-Americans who had migrated north in search of better pay and more opportunities.

In Long Branch, New Jersey, in 1924, hooded Klansmen parade through the streets. Membership of the Klan soared during the first half of the decade. Its revival came at a time when anti-immigrant feelings were running high and many associated "Americanism" with being white and Protestant.

believes, too, that Americanism can only be achieved if the pioneer stock is kept pure." In addition to the supremacy of the Caucasian race, the Klan believed it was their duty to uphold the moral order. The Klan ideals were State, School, Home, and Church.

Their cryptic language, dramatic robes, and elaborate pageantry were typical of fraternal organizations of the time, though they were a bit more flamboyant than most. Many men were drawn to the idea of a secret service that spied on radicals and other threats to society. It especially held excitement for those bored by small town life.

Klan membership increased dramatically with the help of the Southern Publicity Association. The SPA devised a system whereby membership salesmen (kleagles) were allowed to keep four dollars of the ten dollar initiation fee (klecktoken).

With this initiative, the kleagles fanned across the country, especially the rural South, recruiting klansmen by playing upon whatever bigotry and prejudices were present in a particular area. Though most people were horrified by the rise of the Klan, thousands of others were so in agreement with the Klan's crusade to "preserve the old virtues" that they sent in applications.

Some members were not satisfied with burning crosses and parading in hooded sheets. These militant klansmen began a reign of terror in the Southwest. Vigilante squads were formed to punish those who were deemed a threat to society, such as adulterers, radical aliens, and lawyers who represented black clients. The nightriders whipped, tarred and feathered, or lynched their victims.

Imperial wizard Hiram Evans, with the aid of super salesman Edward Clark, made a very successful job of increasing Klan membership in the Southwest. For political reasons Evans favored a more mainstream look for the KKK, and, as lynchings and floggings decreased, Klan membership increased. By 1924, the KKK had over four million members. For the next three years, the KKK played a part in electing state legislators, sheriffs, mayors, senators, and governors around the country. Grand Dragon of the Indiana Realm of the Klan David C. Stephenson claimed, "I am the law in Indiana," and he was pretty much right, for the Klan had helped elect the governor of Indiana, the mayor of Indianapolis, and other political figures.

Ironically, it was Stephenson who helped bring about the decline of the Klan. In 1925, he was convicted of second-degree murder. The victim of the brutal crime was a female secretary from the Indiana statehouse. Mainstream Klan members who believed that the Klan's mission was to uphold American morals and virtues were horrified by the shocking details of the case. When the politicians that Stephenson supposedly had in his back pocket didn't come to his rescue, he sought revenge by squealing on them. Several political figures were arrested for bribery and other charges.

Regardless of the Stephenson scandal, the Klan's political power was about to reach its limit. By persecuting blacks, Jews, Catholics, and all foreign-born people, the Klan had ruled out the support of approximately half of the U.S. population. Some have also argued that the Klan lost its momentum after the Immigration Act of 1924 took effect, thereby accomplishing a main goal of the Klan and taking away one of its rallying cries. In any case, by the end of 1925, the Klan's rise to power, at least for now, was over.

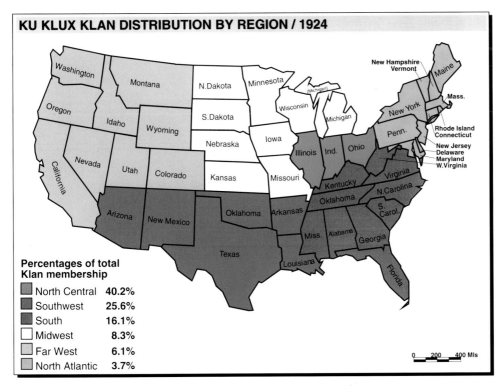

KU KLUX KLAN DISTRIBUTION BY REGION / 1924

Percentages of total Klan membership

North Central	**40.2%**
Southwest	**25.6%**
South	**16.1%**
Midwest	**8.3%**
Far West	**6.1%**
North Atlantic	**3.7%**

This map shows the uneven popularity of the Klan in 1924.

CHAPTER 3
Warren Harding and the
Return to Normalcy

The 1920 Election

President Warren G. Harding with a delegation of women supporters at an April 1921 disarmament conference. A tall, handsome, and likeable man, Harding looked every inch a president. Nevertheless, his administration would later be dogged by stories of scandal and corruption.

Though there was not yet a two-term limit on the presidency in 1920, Wilson was quite obviously too ill to seek another term. Yet at times, he seemed to desire the Democratic nomination. Instead it went to Governor James M. Cox of Ohio. His running mate was the popular assistant secretary of the navy, Franklin D. Roosevelt.

At the Republican convention, a deadlock developed between General Leonard Wood and Illinois Governor Frank O. Lowden. As a result of this, an undistinguished senator from Ohio named Warren G. Harding won the nomination. Then, in an event that would be impossible at today's pre-planned conventions, the delegates surprised Republican leaders by emotionally nominating Calvin Coolidge, of Boston police strike fame, as vice president.

Harding was from Marion, Ohio, where he and his wife Florence had built a small town newspaper into a prosperous enterprise. Though Florence was said to have high political ambitions for her husband, she

was actually satisfied when he reached the U.S. Senate. Harding himself thought his chances were small when he sought the nomination. But his handsome looks and friendly demeanor won over delegates and voters alike.

Harding was elected by an over-whelming margin of almost two to one over Cox. Certainly the high inflation and deep recession moti-vated Americans to vote for change. Although Wilson was a strong leader during the war, many felt that it was the lack of peacetime leadership that was causing so much suffering. The result was a predominant anti-Wilson, anti-Democrat attitude among the public. But perhaps what most drew voters to Harding was his vague, pla-cating speeches, a welcome change from Wilson's sermons about duty to the country and the League of Nations. Harding said just what the people wanted to hear when he declared, "America's first need is not heroics, but healing; not nostrums, but normalcy; not revolution, but restoration . . . not surgery, but seren-ity." He spoke of responsibility, con-ciliation, and tranquility, and it was music to American ears.

The Harding Administration

The decisions Harding made in setting up his cabinet reveal two differ-ent sides to his personality. Some of his appointments were obviously made as the result of careful thought and good intentions, while others reveal poor judgement caused by a misplaced sense of loyalty. For secretary of commerce, Harding chose the well-respected Herbert Hoover, and for secretary of state, he selected the equally admired Charles Evans Hughes. Both men would serve him well.

On the other hand, for secretary of the interior, Harding appointed Albert B. Fall of New Mexico, based solely on the friendship they had formed in the Senate. Perhaps his most disastrous appointment was Harry M. Daugherty, a combative lawyer from Ohio, as attorney gen-eral. Though Harding was warned against it, he felt obligated by loyalty to give his former campaign manager whatever position he wanted. Both Fall and Daugherty would disgrace the Harding administration.

Resolving the War

Though the war had ended two years earlier, its shadow still hung over the country. The unresolved battle between Wilson and Congress over the Treaty of Versailles had left the United States still technically in a state of war. One of Harding's first actions as president was to sign a reso-lution formally revoking the U.S. declaration of war.

Taking advantage of the antiwar mood, Secretary of State Hughes invited nine nations to a disarmament conference to be held on November 11, 1921. In a speech welcoming the delegations, Harding said, "A world staggering with debt needs its burdens lifted. . . . I can speak officially only for our United States. Our hundred millions frankly want less of arma-ment and none of war." Then Hughes took the floor and shocked everyone by not only proposing huge naval cuts, but proceeding to list the specific ships to be cut. He also called on the nations present to participate

Secretary of State Charles Evans Hughes (left), with the Postmaster General Will Hays. Hughes played an important role in the Washington Disarmament Conference of November 1921. He succeeded in getting an agreement to reduce the naval capability of many of the great sea powers in the hope that this would keep the United States out of future world power struggles.

in a ten-year holiday from the building of warships. The wild cheers in response to Hughes' speech lasted ten minutes, with men weeping and throwing their hats in the air.

The naval treaty that resulted from the Washington Conference sought to end the naval arms race that the major nations had been involved in since the beginning of World War I. And, with a ratio of ship tonnage set at 5 U.S. : 5 United Kingdom : 3 Japan, it was also aimed at containing the Imperial Japanese Navy, which had become a source of concern.

In a further move to heal the wounds of war, Harding set about releasing wartime prisoners who had been jailed for their political beliefs. Among those freed was the well-known Socialist leader Eugene V. Debs, whom Wilson had refused to release. Harding released him on December 24, 1921, so that he could be home for Christmas. Though the Red Scare had died down considerably, some still protested Harding's

actions, including one of his close friends. To him, Harding responded, "I was persuaded in my own mind that it was the right thing to do. . . . I thought the spirit of clemency was quite in harmony with the things we were trying to do here in Washington." True to his word, Harding was attempting to promote compassion and calm in the country.

In foreign affairs, however, compassion and calm were hard to come by as relations were souring among the Allies. Britain and France had taken out loans with the United States during the war and were now having a difficult time making the payments as they tried to rebuild their economies. When the United States refused to dismiss the loans, it was criticized as selfish and miserly. On the American side, the French and British were considered welshers by many.

What the United States did not seem to realize was that by demanding payment on the loans, it was actually hurting its own situation in the long run. The Allies owed the United States about $10 billion. Where did they find the money for their repayments? They turned to Germany and demanded the exorbitant war reparations that they were entitled to under the Treaty of Versailles. As a result, Germany nearly went bankrupt. American investors stepped in and lent Germany $2.5 billion to help rebuild German industry. Germany then made its payments to the Allies, who turned around and made their payments back to the American government. So the United States was essentially having its loans paid off with its own money. The situation would become disastrously clear when the Depression hit and the Allies as well as Germany defaulted on their loans.

On to the Economy

From Wilson, Harding inherited an economy wracked by high unemployment, rocketing inflation, and an enormous national debt. To help him face this dilemma, Harding appointed Andrew Mellon as secretary of the treasury. At age sixty-five, Mellon was one of the three richest men in the country, and as such, Harding trusted his economic know-how completely.

Mellon believed that one of the first moves necessary to get the economy going again was a cut in taxes. It's not surprising that, with his perspective as a millionaire businessman, he believed that tax cuts should most benefit corporations and the wealthy in order to encourage investments and economic development. Just as important as cutting taxes, Mellon

believed, was the need to reduce the massive national debt. In 1914, the debt was $1.2 billion. By 1921, it had grown to $24 billion, largely due to war expenses. In order to control government spending and reduce the debt, Harding created the Bureau of the Budget. Finally, there was a plan to run the government like an efficient business, with a strong budget director to keep spending in line.

By 1922, the economy had rebounded, and by 1923, there was even a labor shortage. The national debt was reduced by about a third. An improved economy added to the already high popularity of Uncle Warren, as he was called. His popularity proved to be almost unshakable, and most Americans stood by him even as the scandals unfolded.

A political cartoon depicting Secretary of the Treasury Andrew Mellon recklessly handing tax reductions to a welcoming public. Appointed into his position in 1921, Mellon immediately set about reducing government spending and cutting taxes paid by corporations and high earners. The rich had a lot to thank Mellon for during this decade. They paid up to one-third less tax in 1926 than they had in 1921.

Attorney General Harry Daugherty attempts to hide the skeletons of scandal in the closet in this political cartoon. The skeletons in question were the illegal activities of Daugherty and other of Harding's old poker buddies known as "The Ohio Gang."

The Scandals

One example of Harding's kind-hearted nature was his decision to create the Veterans Bureau to address the concerns of returning soldiers. In an example of his sometimes poor judgment, he appointed Charlie Forbes to head the bureau. Harding had met Forbes when he was in charge of the development of the Pearl Harbor naval base. Though several of the president's advisors warned him of Forbes' unsavory reputation, Harding was won over by the charming man he had come to know during several games of poker.

Forbes proceeded to plunder the bureau by pocketing a share of the profits from sales of so-called surplus supplies, such as bandages and sheets. He then turned around and cut deals for expensive new supplies, profiting from those transactions as well. As rumors of graft began to circulate, Forbes decided it would be wise to take a little trip to Europe. After learning of a planned Senate investigation, Forbes's chief assistant committed suicide, confirming everyone's suspicions. By the time he was found out, Forbes had cost the taxpayers $200 million. Harding was both furious and despondent. But there was more to come.

The next scandal to hit Washington involved an assistant to Attorney General Daugherty named Jess Smith. Smith was a friendly, overweight, diabetic man who was far out of his league in the important political circles of Washington. But he soon learned to take advantage of his access to power. Along with several other corrupt friends, many from Ohio, Smith operated out of the soon to be infamous "little green house on K Street." It was the place to go for those seeking immunity from prosecution, confiscated bootleg liquor, or access to Justice Department files. It is known that Harding himself sometimes visited the "little green house."

When Harding got wind of the rumors of corruption, he ordered Daugherty to get Smith out of Washington. Smith, despondent over the news that he was being exiled, killed himself. As the latest scandal broke in the press, the men involved were dubbed "The Ohio Gang." Once again, Harding was anguished and enraged. As he told one confidant, "I have no trouble with my enemies. I can take care of my enemies all right. But my damn friends . . . they're the ones that keep me walking the floor nights!"

In 1926, Daugherty was indicted on charges of defrauding the government. His refusal to testify led many to believe that he also profited from the corrupt activities of those around him.

Teapot Dome

The scandal that the Harding administration is perhaps most known for is Teapot Dome, which involved Secretary of Interior Albert Fall. A for-

mer Texas marshal and Rough Rider in the Spanish-American War, Fall cut quite a figure with his wide-brimmed hat, black cape, and handlebar mustache. Early on, Fall justified Harding's confidence in him by making the Interior Department more efficient, but his appointment was still criticized by conservationists who feared he would promote the greater use of natural resources. They were especially worried because the Forestry Division had recently been transferred from Agriculture to Interior. The conservationists kept a close eye on Fall and soon learned that their fears were well-founded. His goal, however, involved not trees but oil.

The oil that Fall had set his sights on was located in three large oil fields that had been set aside as reserves for naval use in case of a shortage. Soon after taking office, Fall began discussing with Secretary of the Navy Edwin Denby the possibility of putting those reserves to use. Denby was convinced that it would be a good idea for two reasons: (1) the possibility that the oil fields were being drained by nearby, privately owned wells; and (2) the growing Japanese naval threat in the Pacific. Oil reserves would be essential should another war erupt. Denby agreed that the Interior would be more effective at leasing the reserves, and in May of 1921, he wrote Harding to ask that the reserves be transferred to the Interior Department. Harding agreed.

Soon afterwards, the Interior Department granted a lease in the Elk Hills, California, reserve to Edward Doheny, who happened to be Fall's former prospecting partner out West. Fall also leased all of Naval Oil Reserve Number Three in Wyoming, known as Teapot Dome, to

Harry F. Sinclair. Rumors quickly spread that Teapot Dome had been leased in secret and without competitive bidding. In response to conservationists' demands for action, the Senate opened an investigation into the leasing of naval reserves.

The investigation was headed by Senator Thomas Walsh of Montana. Like Fall, Walsh was a product of the rugged West, with a handlebar mustache, bushy eyebrows, and a growing determination to arrive at the truth. In testimony, Fall admitted that Teapot Dome had been leased secretly, but explained that it was in the interest of national security to do so. He also revealed that another lease was about to be granted to Doheny's company in exchange for storage

Albert Fall (center, left) congratulates Edward Doheny after the latter was acquitted in 1926 of charges for his part in the Teapot Dome scandal. Fall, accused of taking bribes for the lease of government oil fields, was not so lucky. In 1929 he received a one-year prison sentence and a $100,000 fine. The wealthy businessmen who had bribed him were never punished, prompting the refrain popular at the time — "in America, everyone is assumed guilty until proved rich."

tanks and pipelines to be built on the West Coast and at Pearl Harbor. When asked if he personally benefited from the leases in any way or received any money from Doheny or Sinclair, Fall answered with an unequivocal "No." Sinclair firmly supported Fall's testimony, and at that point the investigation seemed to be leading to a dead end.

But Senator Walsh began receiving information that led him to believe otherwise. He learned that around the time that the leases were granted, some interesting developments took place at Fall's Three Rivers ranch. Fall purchased a neighboring ranch and other land worth over $120,000, and he received some

prize livestock that had been sent from a farm owned by Harry Sinclair. Fall, who had by now resigned, was ordered to reappear before the Senate to explain this sudden wealth. He first lied that the money had come from a friend who was not involved with the naval leases. After that friend broke down and admitted it was a lie, Doheny finally revealed that he had loaned Fall $100,000, but claimed that it was a personal loan between friends and had nothing to do with oil. The investigation also turned up evidence that Sinclair had "loaned" Fall money in the form of Liberty Bonds.

After several claims that he was too ill to appear before the committee again, Fall finally showed up but

The August 1923 funeral procession of Warren Harding through Washington, D.C. His premature death spared him from the further humiliations of his scandal-ridden administration.

refused to testify, invoking his Fifth Amendment rights, which state that people do not have to testify against themselves. It would take the rest of the decade to complete the Teapot Dome trials. In the end, Sinclair and Fall were convicted of different charges, but Doheny was somehow acquitted. Perhaps his millions were intimidating to the jury. Though the American public followed the trials through sensational headlines for a time, they soon tired of the affair. Fall maintained until the end that he acted in the best interests of national security and that he had done no wrong.

Ironically, the United States did eventually benefit from the Fall leases of 1921-22. If it hadn't been for the pipelines, storage tanks, and refined oil available at Pearl Harbor on December 7, 1941, the United States would have been even less prepared to return the Japanese attack.

The President's Last Days

By the summer of 1923, just past the halfway point of Harding's term, he was exhausted, worried, and badly in need of a vacation. Scandals were swirling all around him, prohibition was becoming even more difficult to enforce, and both he and his wife were suffering from ill health. To help take his mind off his problems, the president decided to combine business and pleasure with a trip to Alaska, where some territorial conflicts had developed. But far from getting away from it all, Harding was accompanied on his cross-country train by about seventy people, including doctors, cabinet members, and poker pals. Along the way, he stopped for one speaking engagement after another, and while

on the train, he tried to catch up on paperwork.

One month into the trip, Harding's exhaustion overtook him and he fell ill. In San Francisco, he collapsed. Though the story went out that the president was suffering from food poisoning, his doctors actually suspected a heart ailment. One week later, Harding died. As the presidential train, the *Superb*, made its way back to the capitol with Harding's casket, millions of people waited along the tracks for the opportunity to pay their last respects.

Shortly after he was elected, Harding had admitted to reporters, "I can't hope to be the best president this country's ever had. But if I can, I'd like to be the best-loved." The crowds of mourners that stood for hours by the railroad tracks were proof that Harding did indeed win the love of a great number of Americans. He had presided over the country's evolution from postwar turmoil to peacetime pursuits. And he was in charge when the economy made a tremendous recovery. Though Harding was a probusiness president, he had a sincere concern for the working people. Not long before he died, he achieved a goal that he had long been striving for — the end of the twelve-hour day at U.S. Steel.

Whether due to public apathy, Harding's likeable personality, or both, the scandals that plagued his administration did not seem to reflect badly on Harding in the eyes of the people. In fact, the public's reaction to later revelations of corruption that came out in the Daugherty and Teapot Dome trials was to blame the accusers. Americans seemed protective even of the memory of their Uncle Warren.

"I am not fit for this office and never should have been here."

Warren G. Harding

CHAPTER 4
Keeping Cool with Coolidge

Silent Cal

Vice President Calvin Coolidge was awakened in the middle of the night at his father's rustic home in Plymouth, Vermont, to the news that he was now president of the United States. He took the oath of office by the light of a kerosene lamp, with his father presiding as notary.

When he was vice president, the press liked to joke that Coolidge was "silent in sixteen languages." He had a reputation as a stoic New Englander with Puritan morals and a solid integrity. In short, he was just what the country needed after

> "Mr. Coolidge, what was the first thought that came into your mind when you were told that Mr. Harding was dead and the presidency was yours?"
>
> Charles Hokinson (portrait painter)
>
> "I thought I could swing it."
>
> Coolidge

Those who most benefited from Coolidge's economic policies were the rich, who undoubtedly got richer during the decade. Here, they enjoy themselves in typically twenties style with a "wet lunch" at the exclusive Huntingdon Pool, in Los Angeles.

> "He [Coolidge] looks as if he had been weaned on a pickle."
>
> Alice Roosevelt Longworth, *Crowded Hours*

Harding's freewheeling, scandal-ridden presidency. Though it was true that Coolidge had no fondness for small talk, he was a great conversationalist when among friends and had a dry wit that often showed up in his frequent press conferences. In the White House, he made a policy of opening up the Oval Office at 12:30 to visitors who wished to shake their president's hand. Though his personal style was completely different from Harding's, Coolidge also gained a huge popularity with the American people.

Just over a year after Coolidge took office, voters proved his popularity by electing to keep him there for another four years. His slogans for the 1924 campaign were "Keep Cool with Coolidge" and "Coolidge or Chaos." The opposition did indeed seem to be in chaos, with the divided Democrats failing to capitalize on the Teapot Dome scandal. To add to their problems, the Progressive party put forth a candidate who drained off Democratic votes, thereby assuring a Republican victory. But the three-way race apparently did not engender a great amount of enthusiasm in the American people, for voter turnout was barely over 50 percent.

From 1923 to 1928, the United States experienced an economic boom and increases in living standards that later gave rise to the phrase, "Coolidge Prosperity." Of course, Coolidge was obviously not single-handedly responsible for these developments, and the prosperity did not by any measure reach all segments of society. The biggest gains in income went to the top 6 percent of the population, and the number of millionaires in the country rose from seven thousand in 1914 to thirty-five thousand in 1928. Yet, major economic and cultural changes took place during those years that affected every American.

The Business of America

By 1924, the economy was thriving and so was big business. The businessman was hailed as a modern hero who provided a great service to society by creating jobs and keeping his country strong. Coolidge summed up the feelings of many when he said, "The man who builds a factory builds a temple. . . . The man who works there worships there." Around the country, business service clubs such as the Rotarians were popping up, and business was espoused as the manifestation of the American ideal.

The business environment in the United States was undergoing a significant change. Before the war, Progressives warned that large corporations were a threat to democracy. In 1914, the Federal Trade Commission was formed to prevent monopolies and encourage fair competition so that small businesses would not be pushed out by large ones. But, by the time the war was over, much of the steam had already gone out of the Progressive movement. The Child Labor Act, passed by Congress in 1916, was declared unconstitutional by a hostile Supreme Court two years later. During the twenties, Harding and Coolidge appointed conservative members to the FTC who were friendly to big business and less attentive to the concerns of consumers and small businesses.

Coolidge kept Andrew Mellon as secretary of the treasury and agreed with him that a continued hands-off approach to business would keep the economy strong. Commerce Secretary Herbert Hoover promoted trade associations in the hopes that when companies came together, they would share ideas on how to make their businesses more efficient and agree on a code of ethics. The result, however, was that large manufacturers in the same industry would often bypass fair competition by agreeing on a price scale for their goods. The twenties also brought a huge wave of mergers, with major corporations joining forces and further concentrat-ing their power. For example, between 1919 and 1927, more than thirty-seven hundred public utility companies merged into others and disappeared.

New industries that sprang up helped to propel the economy throughout much of the decade and included the brand-new synthetics industry, motion pictures, radio man-ufacturing, and the manufacturing of light metals such as aluminum. But it was automobile manufacturing that ranked as the most important of all the new industries. A 1923 opinion poll suggested Henry Ford would be a more popular candidate for the

LABOR

For further information see primary source entries on pages

11: 1478-79, 1485-88, 1535-37; **12:** 1655-57

The Builder, *painted by Gerrit A. Beneker in the mid-twenties, symbolizes the rising prosperity in the rising skylines of the nation.*

presidency than Harding himself.

Another reason for business's confidence was the exciting boom in productivity that was taking place. Between 1920 and 1929, manufacturing output rose by an amazing 64 percent. Factories were faster and more efficient than ever, due in large part to the new, electrically powered machines that were replacing the old steam-powered equipment. During the twenties, the electricity-generating stations in the United States doubled their capacity as power hungry factories churned out more and more products.

The faster, more efficient factories translated into cost savings for consumers as prices came down. On the negative side, however, workers became familiar with "technological unemployment" as machines replaced people on the assembly-lines.

Other factors in the productivity boom were the new theories of management that took hold in business. The movement to treat management as a science had begun before the war and continued to grow with enthusiasm through the twenties. Managers studied work processes, sales techniques, budgets, and research and development plans to find ways to make companies more efficient and productive. Schools of management were opened at universities, and many young Americans entering the business world set their sights on becoming a manager.

The Consumer Society

Another field that experienced huge growth in the twenties was advertising. A decade earlier, advertising was considered a questionable and not exactly reputable career choice. But in the twenties, advertising became a respectable profession as business came to realize its vital importance. With so many goods being produced so quickly, the quest for consumers became more urgent than ever. The amount of money spent on advertising skyrocketed from $400 million a year before the war to $2.6 billion in 1929.

Americans were bombarded with advertisements like this urging them to buy more goods. Coolidge himself acknowledged the impact of advertising, saying, "It is the most potent influence in adopting and changing the habits and modes of life, affecting what we eat, what we wear, and the work and play of the whole nation."

Holeproof Hosiery

WOMEN of fashion prefer Holeproof Hosiery because it is beautiful — sheer — exquisite. Its reasonable price and long wear are merely additional advantages.

Leading stores offer Holeproof Hosiery in Silk, Wool, Silk and Wool, Silk Faced, and Lusterized Lisle for men, women and children

HOLEPROOF HOSIERY COMPANY, Milwaukee, Wisconsin
HOLEPROOF HOSIERY COMPANY OF CANADA, Limited, London, Ontario   © H. H. Co.

WASH AWAY FAT
AND YEARS
OF AGE

REDUCE!

WITH

La-Mar Reducing Soap

The new discovery. Results quick and amazing —nothing internal to take. Reduce any part of body desired without affecting other parts. No dieting or exercising. Be as slim as you wish. Acts like magic in reducing double chin, abdomen, ungainly ankles, unbecoming wrists, arms and shoulders, large breasts or any superfluous fat on body. Sold direct to you by mail, postpaid, on a money-back guarantee. Price 50c a cake or three cakes for $1.00; one to three cakes usually accomplish its purpose. Send cash or money-order today. You'll be surprised at results.

LA-MAR LABORATORIES
565-A Beckman Building,   Cleveland, O.

Modern advertising was more persuasive than ever. Gone were the sober ads presenting factual information with simple black type. The new ads used hard sell techniques that played on the consumers' emotions and vulnerabilities, especially in regard to social status and personal appearance. The worries of women were a common target, as in the Palmolive ad that shows a swooning couple and reads:

'You would never guess they are married.' It is only of a clever wife that this is ever said. . . . People have changed, and ideals have changed. The 'middle-aged' woman is conspicuously absent in the modern scheme of things.

In her place we have the woman who values the social importance of youth — and keeps it.

The message is if you want to keep your husband, you'd better use Palmolive.

Other ads warned of the dangers of newly elevated medical menaces such as dandruff, halitosis, and pyorrhea. An ad for Forhan toothpaste claimed: "Pyorrhea steals upon you like a thief in the night. . . . Pyorrhea seizes four out of five!" With the rise of the radio and mass magazines in the twenties, consumers were even besieged in their own homes by ads urging them to buy, buy, buy!

And where to get the money for all of these products that the modern American needed? For more and more consumers, the answer was, "Buy now, pay later!" During the twenties, there was a huge increase in installment selling as it became more acceptable to take on personal debt in order to achieve the desired lifestyle. Why wait, the reasoning went, when you could have the furniture, washing machine, or whatever it was that you wanted, right now?

This was a new attitude for the American consumer. In the past, most purchases were paid for with cash, and anyone who would regularly go into debt in order to buy something that could only decrease in value was considered a fool. But the automobile helped change all that. Dealers who were eager to turn over the cars on their showroom floor encouraged buyers to pay in installments, and the idea quickly caught on. By the late twenties, the vast majority of big ticket items were bought on credit, and personal debt in the United States was rising much faster than incomes.

(Left) This advertisement of 1924 was one of many offering miracle cures for what were perceived to be physical shortcomings.

329

"Does your husband

misbehave

grunt and grumble

rant and rave

shoot the brute some

Burma-Shave."

From a 1920s
advertisement

*These diagrams show the
extent of the 1920s auto-
mobile boom.*

Certainly many Americans felt a little guilty about borrowing on the future, but everything would turn out fine, they reasoned, as long as the income kept coming in.

The Amazing Automobile

The auto changed much more than consumer habits during the twenties — it dramatically altered the American lifestyle and landscape. What had been considered a luxury item was quickly becoming a necessity for millions of U.S. citizens. The number of cars and trucks on the road almost tripled during the twenties, reaching just over 26,500,000 in 1929.

It therefore comes as no surprise that the auto industry was a main source of Coolidge Prosperity. The steel, rubber, and glass industries were all propped up by the auto industry,

and it created nearly five million jobs, either directly or indirectly.

With more cars came the need for more and better roads, and those demands were answered. The 1921 Federal Highways Act oversaw the construction of forty-three thousand miles of new roads by 1927, incorporating a system that gave east-west roads even numbers and north-south roads odd numbers. A federal provision granted money to states that would connect their roads to the roads of other states. The famous Route 66 — the great diagonal highway running from Chicago to Los Angeles — was opened in 1926. Alongside those new roads, garages, filling stations, restaurants, and motels popped up to service the adventurous new auto travelers.

Of course, drivers soon became familiar with that other modern invention, the traffic jam. Urban engineers rose to the challenge by

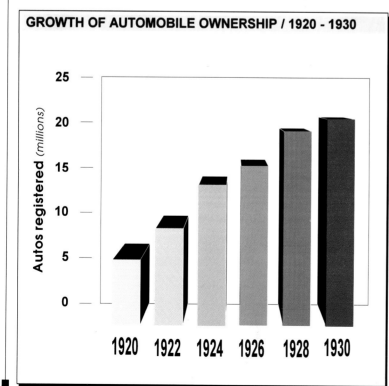

GROWTH OF AUTOMOBILE OWNERSHIP / 1920 - 1930

Autos registered (millions)

25
20
15
10
5
0

1920 1922 1924 1926 1928 1930

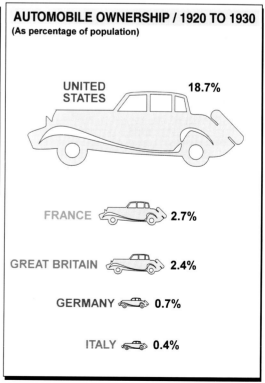

AUTOMOBILE OWNERSHIP / 1920 TO 1930
(As percentage of population)

UNITED STATES   18.7%

FRANCE   2.7%

GREAT BRITAIN   2.4%

GERMANY   0.7%

ITALY   0.4%

This December 1, 1925 photograph shows the first concrete, four-lane super highway, built between Detroit and Pontiac, Michigan. This was one of many highways built in the twenties to accommodate the increasing number of autos on America's roads.

building an incredible array of tunnels, bridges, and clover leaf intersections around the country to help along the ever increasing flow of cars. The first traffic signals were introduced, among them an experimental system in Boston that used a dozen colored lights including purple, blue, and white to direct drivers. That experiment failed.

The first automobile produced at an affordable price for the middle class was the Model T. Henry Ford introduced the Tin Lizzy in 1908 with a price tag of around $850. By 1927, he had lowered the price to under $300 by so perfecting the assembly-line that it could turn out ten thousand cars per week. The growing used-car market was also making the automobile affordable for most families.

The Model T was a huge success, accounting for about 60 percent of all auto sales, but by the middle of the decade, consumers wanted more from a car. Jokes and sayings about the Tin Lizzy were standard around the country, such as "Of all the noises there is none worse, than a Model T Ford when it's in reverse." Henry Ford supposedly said, "Give 'em any color they want, so long as it's black." But jokes aside, drivers were tired of having to stand in the cold and rain to crank the engine, tired of guessing how much gas was in the tank, and definitely tired of black. Though up until the early twenties Ford had maintained a stranglehold on the automobile market, his position as the leader was seriously threatened by innovative challengers, especially General Motors. Alfred P. Sloan, president of GM, was astute enough to realize that the changing demands on the auto industry favored the challenger. As he recalled in his memoirs, "We had no stake in the old ways of the automobile business; for us, change meant opportunity." In

ECONOMY

For further information see primary source entries on pages

11: 1526–28, 1537–39, 1550–53; **12:** 1611–12, 1680–81, 1702–03, 1722–26

Henry Ford. (1863-1947)

As the richest man in the world, Henry Ford may have seemed an unlikely candidate for folk hero status, but common folk across the country embraced "Uncle Henry" and considered him one of their own. Raised on a farm (though he hated farming for himself as a kid), Ford was a self-trained engineer who held many of the same values and beliefs of the working class and rural people who admired him. He believed in hard work, didn't trust bankers, and loved the land.

Ford won the loyalty of many workers by leading the rest of industry in increasing wages and shortening hours. But his motives were practical, rather than humanitarian. The dreary, repetitive work of the assembly line would cause a high rate of turnover in employees unless they were paid well. Ford also believed that mass production would fail without mass consumerism. He explained: "Low wages are silly. You can't get rich by making people poor. They can't buy your goods and there you are." Though generous when paying wages, Ford was not averse to using underhand tactics to stamp out unionism amongst his workers. His "sociological department" even sent spies into the homes of workers he suspected of harboring union sympathies.

In the business-worshipping atmosphere of the twenties, Ford enjoyed a huge popularity. The Ford for president movement that began in 1916 was revived from 1920 to 1923, with clubs springing up around the country. Though Ford never announced his candidacy, he didn't discourage the support either. But when Harding died in 1923, Ford threw his support to Coolidge, leaving his supporters feeling abandoned.

Ford was not without his detractors. In 1919, he bought a newspaper called the *Dearborn Independent* to use as a vehicle for airing his views on the world. In 1920, the paper printed a collection of articles that blamed the Jewish people of the world for everything from the Black Sox scandal to labor unrest. Though Ford later apologized, his reputation was tarnished.

The stock market crash of 1929 came as no surprise to Ford, who had long claimed that speculation was getting out of hand and had no basis in reality. In the Depression that followed, Ford's popularity inevitably declined as he, like most business leaders, was forced to cut wages and lay off workers.

contrast to Ford's static models, GM made yearly improvements on its models and offered a bigger package of accessories. Under Sloan's leadership, GM wooed away Ford customers by promising more for their money, including more leg room, automatic windshield wipers, a rainbow of brilliant colors, and other options. In 1927, Ford answered back with the Model A, the unveiling of which caused enormous excitement throughout the country. In general, the automobile changed quite a bit during the twenties. The open touring cars were replaced by closed cars, and balloon tires were introduced to make auto travel considerably more comfortable.

The automobile changed American life in some obvious and

The fifteen millionth Ford, and almost the last of the Model T's, came off the assembly-line in May 1927. Ford's most famous car was soon to be replaced by the Model A, which, unlike the Model T, was offered in a variety of colors.

some not-so-obvious ways. The increased freedom of movement made it easier for people to live further away from their workplace. More and more Americans chose to live in the rapidly growing suburbs and drive to their jobs in the cities. A car also meant newfound freedom for young couples. No longer did they have to do their courting on the front porch or in the parlor, where watchful parents were never far away. And the farmer who owned a car or truck was no longer as isolated as he or she once was. In fact, the automobile made the whole country more accessible to Americans than it had ever been before. Tourists and executives alike began crisscrossing the country, and as a result, regional differences began to melt away.

The United States would continue to feel the tremendous impact of the auto for years to come. The proliferation of highways, gas stations, traffic lights and shopping centers altered the physical landscape and created much of the world we know today. The popular humorist Will Rogers did what he did best when he wryly summed up the situation in a tribute to Henry Ford, the man who started it all: "It will take a hundred years to tell whether you have helped us or hurt us, but you certainly didn't leave us like you found us."

Healthy Developments

The proliferation of the automobile is but one example of the rise in living standards that the twenties brought to the United States. Perhaps even more important are the dramatic improvements in health that took place. Life expectancy rose from fifty-five to sixty, a huge gain for just ten years. The number of deaths due to diphtheria, typhoid, and tuberculosis was drastically reduced, especially in cities and

"His motor car was poetry, tragedy, love and heroism."

Sinclair Lewis,
Babbitt

industrialized states. Infant mortality rates also dropped.

There are several reasons for these improvements, including changes in the average American's diet. The introduction of refrigerated railroad cars and trucks meant that people all over the country could enjoy fruits and vegetables year round, and with the increase in home refrigerators (from 27,000 in 1923 to 755,000 in 1928), families found it easier to keep those healthy foods in stock. In addition, public-health programs in the ever-expanding cities were helping to educate, inoculate, and in general, provide more medical care than ever before. Safer factories and improvements in city water supplies also helped Americans live healthier, longer lives.

Mary McLeod Bethune is shown here in 1936 visiting the mother of President Roosevelt.

Mary McLeod Bethune. (1875-1955)

"With faith, you can make it." So believed Mary McLeod Bethune, and her life did indeed bear out her philosophy. Born in 1875 in South Carolina, she was considered special right from the beginning, for she was the first of Samuel and Patsy McLeod's children to be born free.

From an early age, Mary displayed a sharp intellect and a strong desire to learn. Samuel McLeod was a sharecropper who needed the help of all seventeen of his children to work the land. But when a missionary came looking for students to enroll in a new school for black children, the McLeods decided that Mary should be allowed to fulfill her thirst for knowledge.

Mary's faith came through again four years later when she received a scholarship to continue her studies at Scotia Seminary. After graduation, she married Albertus Bethune and had a child. But instead of settling into domestic life, Mary began to dream of building a school for black children, of spreading the light of education into more young lives.

Mary McLeod Bethune heard that in Daytona, blacks were being hired to lay tracks for a new railroad line in Florida. The living conditions were miserable, and no schooling was provided for the children. She decided that Daytona was the place for her school. Bethune arrived in town with $1.50 and a dream. In 1904, she opened the Daytona Normal School and Industrial Institute for Negro Girls with five students, who used charcoal for pencils and berries for ink. By 1905, the school had grown to one hundred students and included living quarters.

Bethune's radiating enthusiasm drew others into her dream and persuaded them to take part in helping it grow. She used her creative talents to find ways to raise money to keep her school afloat, such as staging performances of the school's choir. As the school grew, so did its needs. Bethune began looking for patrons among the wealthy people on the "other side of the tracks." Among the school's contributors was John D. Rockefeller and J. G. Gamble of the Proctor and Gamble company. Bethune was so persuasive that one sponsor said of her, "If she gets you cornered, you might as well reach for your pocketbook."

In 1925, The School, as it was simply known, merged with Cookman College to become the coeducational Bethune-Cookman College, which exists to this day. In later years, Bethune achieved further prominence, including an appointment in the Roosevelt administration. She became friends with Eleanor Roosevelt, working with her to promote the concerns of women and the young.

Mary McLeod Bethune proved that when faith is combined with hope and determination, dreams can be realized.

The Education Explosion

During the twenties, an important shift was taking place in Americans' attitudes towards education. Whereas schooling, especially secondary and higher education, had been considered something of a privilege in the past, it was increasingly being seen as a basic right that all Americans, no matter how poor, were entitled to claim. In 1923-24, Helen and Robert S. Lynd studied the town of Muncie, Indiana, incorporating their findings in a book that became a milestone in sociological analysis, called *Middletown*. They observed that, "If education is oftentimes taken for granted by the business class, . . . it evokes the fervor of a religion, a means of salvation, among a large section of the working class." The statistics bear out this truth: The portion of high-school-aged people attending secondary schools soared from 25 percent in 1918 to over 50 percent in 1930. Part of this increase is probably due to the fact that increased mechanization was making children less necessary as workers on the farms and in the factories. In any case, by 1930, all fifty states had instituted compulsory attendance laws.

In order to keep up with the greater demands for education, the nation was spending a billion dollars a year on schools. New schools were built, the school year was extended, and extracurricular activities were offered, giving the school a more influential role in the community.

Other interesting developments were taking place inside the classroom. The Progressive movement of the previous decade espoused ideas for making education more effective and more connected to students' lives. Educator and philosopher John Dewey advocated treating students

> *"Mr. Lincoln had told our race we were free, but mentally we were still enslaved."*
>
> *"For I am my mother's daughter, and the drums of Africa still beat in my heart. They will not let me rest while there is a single Negro boy or girl without a chance to prove his worth."*
>
> Mary McLeod Bethune

The number of children in school increased significantly during the 1920s. New schools often possessed a gymnasium and a science laboratory, a far cry from the one-room schoolhouses of previous decades.

as individuals by recognizing their distinct personalities and abilities. He also believed that less emphasis should be placed on rote learning and more placed on problem solving. In part because of these theories, educators began trying experimental new methods of teaching in an attempt to update the schools for the modern world. Of course, these changes did not come without controversy. Critics complained that discipline was being sacrificed and basic subjects were losing ground to physical education, shop class, and other electives.

Expanding Cities

The United States was rapidly becoming an urbanized nation. In 1920, the national census revealed that for the first time, over half of all Americans lived in communities with a population of twenty-five hundred or more. Though two and a half thousand people does not exactly amount to a bustling city, the statistics show the general shift in population from rural to urban areas that was due in large part to the difficult times in the farming sector during the 1920s. Big cities especially experienced huge growth, and by 1930, Detroit, Los Angeles, New York, Chicago, and Philadelphia all had populations of more than a million.

City governments responded to the increasing demands on their infrastructures by making improvements in their water systems, transportation networks, and other public services. But in the area of housing, the cities fell short. Overcrowded slums were a growing problem in most cities, and they led to other problems, such as increased juvenile delinquency and drug abuse.

Housing conditions in general still had a long way to go. Though automobiles, telephones, and radios were spreading across the country, one-third of the American population was considered badly housed in 1930. Many homes had no electricity, no running water, no bath, and no inside toilet.

Overcrowded slums were a growing urban problem during the twenties as more people moved into the cities. This picture shows African-American children playing in a slum backyard in Cincinnati, Ohio.

The Foreign Policy Front

On the domestic scene, Coolidge seemed to have little to worry about, but foreign affairs were a different story. By 1923, Germany's economy was in a shambles, and it had failed to make the required payments for war damages to France. In response, the French sent in troops to occupy the Ruhr, an industrial region in western Germany. The United States quickly sought to ease tensions. Secretary of State Charles Evans Hughes proposed an international committee to devise a payment schedule for Germany, and France withdrew. But meanwhile, a young Adolf Hitler took advantage of the turmoil and attempted to seize power in the "Beer Hall Putsch," so named because he stirred up a rally of storm-troopers in a Munich beer hall the day before his attempt to overthrow the Bavarian government. He was arrested and jailed for five years.

Closer to home, Latin America was also giving Coolidge cause for concern. Relations between the United States and its neighbors to the south had been deteriorating for years, ever since Theodore Roosevelt's interventionist policies had provoked animosity there. Coolidge sought to improve the situation by extending diplomatic recognition to Mexico in 1923, but the friendly atmosphere soon changed.

In 1925, two developments took place in Mexico that aroused American anger. First, the Mexican government passed a law restricting foreign oil rights in their country, which greatly upset American oil companies. Secondly, they announced plans to nationalize all church property. When Catholic bishops in Mexico resisted nationalization, the government

American-trained Nicaraguan National Guardsmen firing from the top of the national bank building in Managua during the 1926-27 civil war.

cracked down, closing convents and religious schools. American Catholics joined the oil companies in clamoring for Coolidge to take action, but the president remained vague and calm on the subject of Mexico.

That soon changed when a Nicaraguan civil war was thrown into the mix. In December of 1926, the already unstable country broke into civil war between Conservative President Adolfo Diaz's troops and the forces of ousted Vice President Juan Sacasa, a Liberal. Sacasa was aided by a general named Sandino, and their rebels were called Sandinistas. Mexico began supporting Sacasa with arms supplies, and the United States sold arms to Diaz, whom they had helped put in power. Coolidge sent in marines, claiming they were necessary to protect American lives and property in Nicaragua. As a result, tensions between the United States and Mexico were quickly raised to a dangerous level.

Many members of Congress assailed the Coolidge administration for its actions and called for an immediate withdrawal of troops. By March of 1927, Coolidge and Secretary of State Frank Kellogg were looking for a way out of the dilemma. The two sides in Nicaragua had reached a bloody impasse and also seemed ready for peace. Coolidge sent former Secretary of War Henry L. Stimson to Nicaragua to help put an end to the civil war. Soon both sides had agreed to elections in 1928, and the United States began withdrawing forces.

Now attention was turned to repairing relations with Mexico. To aid that effort, Coolidge appointed his old classmate Dwight Morrow as ambassador to Mexico, sending him off with these words: "My only instructions are to keep us out of war with Mexico." Morrow did an excellent job, demonstrating a friendly, cooperative attitude to the Mexicans, rather than the bullying posture of the previous ambassador.

Though there were some very tense moments, Coolidge succeeded in leading the United States through the labyrinth of foreign relations without leading it into war. He even began the process of improving relations with Latin America that would continue with later administrations.

Another foreign relations development that garnered a great deal of attention was the signing of the Kellogg-Briand Treaty, which was ratified by the Senate in January 1929. Under this agreement, over sixty nations, including Japan, Germany, and Italy, pledged that they would not use force against each other. Though the treaty caused a great deal of excitement and many hoped that it would insure world peace, critics pointed out that there was no way to enforce it. Their skepticism would prove to be well-founded as World War II approached.

The 1928 Election

By the summer of 1927, the frenzy leading up to the 1928 election had already begun, including much speculation about whether or not Coolidge would seek reelection. Many Republicans believed he would be a shoo-in if he ran, and many Democrats were fearful of just that.

To Coolidge, however, the pleasure caused by such rosy predictions was diminished by the idea of four more burdensome years in office. The glory of the presidency was gone

President Coolidge is surrounded by other people's guesses of what he has in mind in this political cartoon.

almost from the start for Coolidge, when tragedy struck the White House in 1924. Coolidge's son, Calvin, Jr., died from blood poisoning that began with a blister on his toe. He was sixteen years old. For the remainder of his term, Coolidge quietly grieved. In less personal matters, Coolidge had begun to worry about the stability of Coolidge Prosperity amid reports of excessive speculation on the stock market.

On August 2, 1927, Coolidge held a press conference in a high school math classroom. As the reporters filed in, he gave each one a slip of paper on which were typed the words, "I do not choose to run for president in nineteen twenty-eight." There was no explanation, no comment. The reporters scrambled from the room to call in their stories.

In this instance, Coolidge certainly lived up to his nickname, "Silent Cal," for even his own wife did not know of his decision until after he had told the press.

Herbert Hoover easily won the Republican nomination, and the still-divided Democrats chose New York Governor Alfred E. Smith. Hoover won in a landslide, primarily on the pledge of continued Republican prosperity. (It was a Republican campaigner who wrote the famous promise of "a chicken in every pot.")

Al Smith. (1873-1944)

The grandson of Irish immigrants, Alfred Emanuel Smith was born in the slums of Manhattan's Lower East Side. As a young man, Smith worked hard at various unskilled jobs. He also became involved with Tammany Hall, the fraternal order that was the Democratic power base in the city. The Tammany leaders groomed Smith for higher and higher positions, finally helping him become governor of New York in 1918. Though he lost a bid for reelection in 1920 (when it was still a two-year term), he won back the office in 1922 and served as governor until 1928.

Smith never forgot his humble beginnings and pushed for progressive legislation to help the common working people, such as a minimum wage and maximum hours for working women and children. He reorganized New York government to make it more effective and less wasteful, earning a reputation as a decisive legislator.

What made Smith most popular was his winning personality. Formerly an amateur actor, Smith was a dramatic and sincere speaker. He liked a good joke and occasionally broke into song if the mood was right and there was an audience.

When Smith decided to run for president in 1928, the limits to his popularity became glaringly clear. Rural Americans made up about half the population, and many of them were decidedly suspicious of the city man with his expensive suits and East Side accent. Though Smith said that, as president, he would uphold all of the laws of the land, he proclaimed that what the country needed was not prohibition but temperance when it came to alcohol. In the vicious atmosphere of the election, false rumors spread that Smith was a boozer.

But the biggest strike against Smith was his Catholicism. One Methodist bishop pulled no punches, claiming: "No governor can kiss the papal ring and get within gunshot of the White House." A Manhattan lawyer used a more restrained approach, asking in the *Atlantic* whether or not Smith would have to answer to the Pope if he were in the White House. With the help of aides, Smith prepared a response which read in part:

"I recognize no power in the institutions of my church to interfere with the Constitution of the United States or the enforcement of the law of the land ... I join with fellow Americans of all creeds in a fervent prayer that never again in this land will any public servant be challenged because of the faith in which he has tried to walk humbly with his God." Smith later came to resent the successful rise of his gubernatorial successor Franklin D. Roosevelt. He became an opponent of the New Deal and gave his support to Republican candidates who opposed Roosevelt in the 1936 and 1940 elections.

But another large factor in the defeat of Al Smith was the fact that he was a Catholic. Though the Klan was virtually dead by 1928, a lingering prejudice against Catholics still led many Americans to believe that Smith had no place in the White House.

CHAPTER 5
Tough Times for Farmers and Workers

Left Out of Coolidge Prosperity

Though business was booming and stock market speculators were making fortunes overnight, not everyone in the twenties went about singing "We're in the Money." Certain segments of the population were left out of the Coolidge Prosperity, including farm families, who were familiar with the term *Depression* even before the thirties began.

The tumbledown home of an Arkansas sharecropper and his family in the 1920s. Sharecroppers were farmers who exchanged a share of their crops in return for the use of land and money to buy their tools and seeds. Sharecroppers were near the bottom of the agricultural ladder and were often in debt, as the proceeds from the crops they raised were barely enough to cover their rent and loans.

The Farmers' Plight

As the twenties began, the United States was still largely an agricultural nation, with one-third of the population relying on farming for its livelihood. But as the new decade began, that one-third was facing tough times.

During World War I, farmers had borrowed heavily in order to keep up their production to meet the nation's needs and make a profit besides. They eagerly bought up land as well as tractors, electrical millers, and other new machines, going into debt in the process. At the time, the farmers didn't worry much about being able to make payments since the prices for their goods were stable, thanks in large part to government support. But then the war ended, and the government withdrew its price supports. At the same time, the export market went into decline as European nations had less money to buy American crops. With demand down, prices fell and the farmers were left holding more debt than they could carry. Not only were the Europeans buying less, but so were Americans. Plus, synthetic fibers were replacing cotton, and prohibition devastated the market for barley and grapes, the main ingredients in beer and wine.

At the same time, advances were being made in the field of agriculture. Farmers were gaining greater control over crop and animal diseases, and better, heartier strains were being developed. New machinery was making farming much safer and more

A John Deere tractor and plow of the early 1920s. Farmers borrowed heavily to buy the new farm machinery at a time when farm prices were falling dramatically. As a result, many were forced to sell out, pay off their debts, and then leave the land for good.

productive. In 1921, 1922, and 1923, American farmers had bumper crops, which was the last thing they needed, since huge crops created a glut on the market. Prices continued to tumble. Some farmers attempted to keep their goods off the market until they could get a decent price for them, but the banks tried to force the farmers to sell so that they could make payments on their loans.

The bottom fell out for many farm families. They packed up their Model T's with their belongings and headed for the towns and cities. During the twenties, the total number of farms in the United States decreased for the first time in the nation's history.

A Search for Solutions

The farmers who stayed behind became desperate for a way out of their troubles. They turned to the government for help. The American Farm Bureau Federation became a powerful lobbying force in Washington, and a group of Congressmen known as the farm bloc sought to pass laws that would offer relief to farmers. They helped enact the Farmers' Loan Act of 1923 to ease the repayment schedules on farm loans. They pushed for a high tariff to lessen competition from foreign markets. They supported the Federal Highways Act so that farmers could get their goods to market more easily and quickly. But still, many farmers were barely making ends meet.

In 1924, two executives from a plow company proposed to the farm bloc an idea for a bill based on the idea of "Agricultural Equality." The executives were George N.

Peek and Hugh S. Johnson, who said, "You can't sell a plow to a busted customer." Under the McNary-Haugen bill, named after the Congressmen who advanced it, the government would buy the farmers' surplus goods and dump them on foreign markets in order to help keep prices high at home. The plan was that increased profits at home would make up for the money lost during the dumping process. For the rest of the decade, the McNary-Haugen bill would be a stormy issue.

Though many farmers were enthusiastically for it, critics pointed out that the plan was based on flawed logic. By keeping prices high at home, farmers would be encouraged to keep up production, and the problem of surplus goods would never be solved. Coolidge urged patience. He, along with many others, advised the farmers to cooperate with each other and adjust their production to the needs of the market. The president was worried about what the bill would do to the federal budget, which he had been steadfastly trying to reduce. But he also worried that if the plan were carried out, foreign countries would retaliate by dumping *their* goods on the U.S. market and raising *their* tariffs, which would only add to the problems of the American farmer.

The McNary-Haugen bill was twice passed and twice vetoed by Coolidge. In his second veto message, Coolidge wrote, "There is no thoughtful man who does not fully appreciate how vital a prosperous agriculture is to this nation. It must be helped and strengthened. To saddle it with unjust, unworkable schemes of governmental control is

343

to invite disaster worse than any that has yet befallen our farmers." Meanwhile, the stream of farm families escaping to the cities continued.

Labor's Dilemma

Organized labor was another group that did not fare well in the twenties. During the progressive Wilson administration and especially during the war, labor had made great strides, with labor leaders even attaining government positions. In 1920, union membership in the United States reached just over five million. Though this was still only a small portion of the total number of wage earners in the United States, it represented a high point for organized labor. For the rest of the twenties, it would all be downhill.

By 1920, big business was tired of attacks from progressive reformers and felt that the unions had gone far enough. Industrialists especially didn't like the idea of collective bargaining, which they felt took all the power away from owners and put it in the hands of unions. Now business was ready to fight back.

In 1921, the National Association of Manufacturers announced the beginning of "the American Plan."

The 1926 skyline of Pittsburgh, Pennsylvania, was typical of many industrial cities of this decade. Big business was organizing to restrict the power of the unions, whose membership decreased through the 1920s.

The stated purpose of the plan was to do away with closed shops, companies where only union members could be employed. The unstated purpose was union-busting and strike-breaking. The president of NAM, John Edgerton, branded closed shops as un-American, claiming that they were an assault on individualism. He spoke for many in industry when he declared, "I am unalterably opposed to the present form in which so-called labor is organized."

To keep "so-called labor" from organizing any further, companies planted spies in their factories who kept management informed of any union rumblings. One member of the American Federation of Labor pointed out that there were two pages of private detective agencies listed in the Chicago telephone book. Another method for beating unions was to hire strike-breakers to cross picket lines. Unlike scabs who were brought in to permanently fill the strikers' positions, strike-breakers were often thugs with criminal records who came in just long enough to put an end to the strike. Private police forces were also hired by large companies to keep order during strikes. Of course, unlike public police forces, these men were not assigned to provide equal protection under the law, but rather to guard the company's interest. The Pennsylvania Coal and Iron Police, like others, were notorious for often resorting to violence and beating strikers.

In 1918, Republican majorities were elected to both the House and the Senate, and two years later, the pro-business Harding was voted into the White House. By 1920, friends of labor were hard to come by in Washington. The Justice Department also showed little sympathy for unions. In 1921, the Supreme Court severely restricted the rights of strikers to peacefully picket, and throughout the country, courts ordered injunctions against union activities. Some injunctions made it illegal for strikers to publicize their strike, to meet to plan strategy, and even to come within a mile of the plant they were striking against.

A Position of Weakness

Organized labor found itself unprepared to respond to the challenges it faced. As mentioned earlier, the percentage of unionized workers in the United States was relatively small even at its high point. In other countries, the industrial revolution had created strong labor movements. But U.S. workers seemed to have more difficulty organizing. One reason was that a large part of the work force in the United States was made up of immigrants, many of whom were willing to work under horrible conditions in order to survive. They also spoke a multitude of languages, making organization on a large scale almost impossible. During the twenties, farmers and southern blacks were moving to the industrialized cities in droves, but rather than adding their numbers to the unions' strength, they only diluted it. Many unions refused to accept blacks at all and, even in those that did, there was often a high degree of racial segregation by task and working conditions. Farmers were in the habit of relying on themselves, and their philosophy of individualism made them unlikely union members. As for African-Americans, most unions let prejudice get in the

Black firefighters in Indianapolis, 1926. Many African-Americans were drawn to the North by the prospect of better pay. They moved into the big cities where many took service jobs, such as firefighting, or became meat packers, auto workers, or metal workers.

way of self-interest and shut out their black coworkers.

As machines replaced workers in factories, they added to the strength of business and the weakness of labor. Though the Department of Labor did a horrible job of recording accurate unemployment statistics during the twenties, estimates figure the average rate for the decade to be about 10 percent. It was much higher in cer-

tain industries. Strikes were difficult to organize with the majority of workers grateful to have any job, no matter how bad it was.

Adding to the labor movement's problems from within, business did its best to undercut the power of the unions. One method they used was the company union, created by management and offered as an alternative to trade unions. To the employers,

Station # 1. 1926.

this was the better alternative, since it allowed the employees within the company to organize but didn't allow them to join with other workers from other companies. Though these unions did not have the right to strike or order work stoppages, they did offer a way for workers to air their grievances. As a result, health and safety conditions improved in some cases. But skeptical workers did not consider these to be real unions and often referred to them as "Kiss Me Clubs."

Whether business was seeking to steal the unions' thunder or to really improve labor relations, the idea of "welfare capitalism" was much talked about during the twenties. Some companies even did more than talk. The idea was that workers should no longer be considered as mere commodities but should be encouraged to have an interest in the firm. The hoped-for result was a more loyal and productive employee. Welfare capitalism plans included popular benefits such as life insurance, employee stock-ownership, and rent assistance.

Only a small number of profitable firms enacted welfare capitalism, and the benefits reached a limited group of workers. But still they had the effect of making trade unions appear

President Harding relaxes with inventor and businessman, Thomas Edison (second from left), Henry Ford (far left) and others. Public admiration for successful businessmen grew in the 1920s.

less and less necessary, and public opinion began tilting away from organized labor. One of the city leaders in *Middletown* explains: "Working men don't need unions nowadays. There are no great evils or problems now as there were fifty years ago. We are much more in danger of coddling the working men than abusing them." During the twenties it was the successful businessmen who won the public's admiration; people like Henry Ford and J.P. Morgan.

Unions were also still looked on by many with a lingering suspicion of communism. In 1922, a strong brotherhood of railroad workers went on strike after wage cuts were proposed. Trucks and cars had been cutting deeply into the railway business, resulting in major losses. Attorney General Daugherty insisted that it was all part of a Communist plot to force the government to take over the railroads, which would be the beginning of the end for capitalism. The strike ended with nothing to show for the railroad workers.

The Gastonia Strike

One of the most famous strikes of the twenties took place in Gastonia, North Carolina, home of the Loray Mill. As was typical in mill towns, the workers lived in a company-owned, isolated section of Gastonia. Company towns typically provided houses, utilities, stores, and even schools and churches for the employees who lived there. But in exchange for this so-called security, workers gave over control of a huge part of their lives to their employers. A reporter covering a Pittsburgh Coal

strike described the company town there: "We unearthed a system of despotic tyranny reminiscent of Czar-ridden Siberia at its worst. We found . . . industrial slavery."

The mill village was a desperate place, and working conditions in the mill were worse, with average temperatures around ninety degrees and a constant, deafening noise. When the textile industry hit a recession, the parent company of the Loray Mill cut wages, laid off workers, and imposed a "stretch-out" on the mill, which basically meant that the employees' work loads were increased. Adults as well as children were working ten to twelve hours a day and barely making enough to get by.

The Communist-controlled National Textile Workers Union had been planning to move into the southern textile industry and decided that the Loray Mill was a good place to start. In March of 1929, they sent Fred E. Beal into town. Beal began recruiting millworkers into an underground organization, but soon a company spy discovered the plan. When five of the unionized workers were subsequently fired, a strike was organized.

The union presented its demands for higher wages, shorter hours, and better living conditions to the management. They were promptly refused. Furthermore, the union was condemned for having Communist leaders. The company refused to deal with the organization until it denounced communism. The Gastonia newspapers printed ads proclaiming that the strike was called for "the purpose of overthrowing this government and destroying property and to kill, kill,

kill. The time is at hand for every American to do his duty."

The textile workers of Loray Mill had the bad fortune of being organized by a union that was, indeed, led by Communists. When those leaders arrived in Gastonia, the goals of the downtrodden workers were given a back seat to the unrealistic, attention-grabbing objectives of the organizers. The citizens of Gastonia who did not live in the mill town were enraged by the arrival of these outside agitators. Tensions mounted, and on April 18, a mob demolished the union headquarters in the middle of the night. Still the union held on, and when strikers refused to return to work, sixty-two families were evicted from their homes. (Some accounts put the number at over one hundred families.) A tent city was erected to house the

Home of a depressed industry, where pay and conditions were already poor, Loray Mill, Gastonia, North Carolina, became a focal point for the activities of the National Textile Workers Union. Ellen Dawson of New Jersey, an outside agitator, is here seen addressing the striking mill workers. She was later arrested by the U.S. marshal.

AMERICA IN THE 20TH CENTURY: 1920 - 1929

Fred E. Beal. (1896-1954)

At the age of fourteen, Fred Beal went to work in the textile mills, and it was there that he first became a believer in the power of unions. In 1912, he joined a strike organized by the Industrial Workers of the World, who were roused by the speeches of IWW leader Big Bill Haywood.

After serving in World War I, Beal tried various left wing organizations. He eventually joined the Communist party in 1928, but Beal was never a devoted convert to communism. He believed the party leaders were incompetent, and considered their propaganda efforts with skepticism: "When we [the workers] got their pamphlets and papers, full of such words as proletariat, ideological, aggrandizement, manifestations, capitulate and orientate, we pretended to understand what it all meant, and let it go at that." Still, Beal believed that the Communist party was the only organization committed to the workers.

When Beal was sent by the Communist-led National Textile Workers Union to Gastonia, North Carolina, he had high hopes of organizing one of the most powerless groups of workers in the country. But the strike disintegrated into violence, and the chief of police was killed. In October 1929, faced with a sentence of twenty years at hard labor for second-degree murder, Beal finally took the opportunity to see for himself the "workers' paradise" that he had heard so much about by taking a trip to the Soviet Union.

What he found was more like Hell. Beal was disillusioned by the beggars, the many orphans, and the corruption within the party. He managed to return to the United States only to find more beggars in his native country as the Depression was in full swing. Once again, he returned to the Soviet Union to give it another chance. But this time, he discovered unimaginable horrors, with Stalin's troops slaughtering millions of so-called wealthy peasants.

In 1933, Beal escaped from the USSR. He returned to the United States and lived underground for five years. During that time, he wrote his autobiography in which he attacked Bolshevism and the Communist party. Eventually, the police caught up with Beal, and he was imprisoned. His choice between the two countries was finally made as he declared: "I would rather be an American prisoner than a free man in Russia."

Fred E. Beal is carried on the shoulders of enthusiastic Communists after his return from trial at Charlotte for the murder of Chief of Police O.F. Aderholt.

homeless families and provide for a new union headquarters.

Soon afterwards, a fight broke out during a demonstration at the mill. The police were called, and a gun battle erupted. When it was over, one striker and four policemen were hit. Among them was Police Chief O. F. Aderholt, who was fatally wounded.

Sixteen strikers were charged with conspiracy leading to murder. At the trial, a lawyer for the prosecution somehow planned to prove a point by dramatically unveiling a bloody replica of the murdered policeman. The widow, her daughter, and one of the jurors became hysterical, and a mistrial was called.

When the people of Gastonia heard that the trial had ended without convictions for the strikers, mob violence ensued. After several strikers were assaulted and almost lynched, the union planned a rally to protest. An integral member of most union gatherings was a twenty-five-year-old millworker named Ella May Wiggins. She was known for her simple ballads that described the millworkers' desperate lives and their determination to fight for better:

How it grieves the heart
of a mother,
You every one must know.
For we can't buy for our
children,
Our wages are too low.

On the way to the rally, a truckload of strikers, including Wiggins, was forcibly stopped and then riddled with

National Guardsmen on duty in the grounds of the Loray Mill in Gastonia. They were called in after threats had been received that Communist-led workers were planning to destroy the mill.

gunfire. Wiggins was the only one killed. Though there were over fifty witnesses to the murder, the five vigilantes charged with the crime were found not guilty.

In the second trial of the strikers, which were now down to seven since charges were dropped on the other nine, the jury took less than an hour to reach a verdict. All seven were convicted, receiving sentences ranging from five to twenty years. Acting on advice from the party in Moscow,

Fred Beal and the others fled to the "workers' paradise" in Russia while they were out on bail.

The strike in Gastonia is representative of the fate of organized labor in the United States by the end of the twenties. Repressed by strong-arm business tactics, maligned in the press, and lacking good leadership, the unions were deteriorating. From five million in 1920, membership had fallen by about one and a half million by 1929.

A typical home of a striking worker, this time from the mills of the American Bemberg and Glanzstoff Corporations at Elizabethton, Tennessee.

CHAPTER 6
The Nation at Play

The Hyper Decade

As the postwar tensions that marked the beginning of the twenties began to fade, Americans turned their attention to the pursuit of pleasure. And oh, how they pursued it! The emotional energy that was generated during the war seemed to spill over into the search for diversions. Within ten years, spending on recreation and amusement rose by 300 percent.

As the recession of 1920-21 came to an end, people had more money to spend and more leisure time on their hands. As electricity reached more and more homes, an increasing number of women took advantage of new, time-saving appliances, such as vacuum cleaners and washing machines. And with the proliferation of refrigerators and bakeries, less time was spent on chores such as canning and baking. So, with time and money to spare, Americans went looking for a good time.

As electricity reached more and more homes in the twenties, the market for electrical goods, like vacuum cleaners and washing machines, expanded. The trick of the salesperson was to persuade the public they needed the new appliances that were on offer.

The Dream Palace

The Paramount Theatre, New York, was one of the grandest of the new "dream palaces." Opened in 1926, it provided seating for four thousand people.

Throughout the twenties, Americans flocked to movie theaters in ever-increasing numbers. Movies, especially the silents, held universal appeal. Charlie Chaplin's tramp was just as funny to the middle-class businessman as he was to the immigrant who could barely understand English. What's more, motion pictures offered the luxury of escape, a point high-lighted in this advertisement from the *Saturday Evening Post*: ". . . . All the adventure, all the romance, all the excitement you lack in your daily life are in — Pictures. They take you

completely out of yourself into a wonderful new world. . . ."

In the previous decade, movies were a novelty, and the sight of moving pictures projected on a screen kept audiences spellbound. Most films were highly emotional and earnest, though they had an unpolished look about them. During the twenties, the movies changed. Wall Street tycoons were eager to get a piece of the action, and soon movies became part of the big business trend. Like all good managers, the new studio heads were motivated by what sells, or in Hollywood lingo, big box office. The idea of formula pictures became popular, based on the theory that if the audience bought it before, they'd buy it again.

Audiences also bought into the star system, and publicity men milked it for all it was worth, sometimes even arranging marriages and divorces between stars to keep the public interested. The publicity machine reached a new high (or low) with the untimely death, in 1926, of the greatest heartthrob of the time, Rudolph Valentino. Thanks to the efforts of

"Valentino had silently acted out the fantasies of women all over the world. Valentino and his world were a dream. A whole generation of females wanted to ride off into a sandy paradise with him."

Bette Davis

Rudolph Valentino, the leading "screen lover" of the twenties. Here, he portrays a gaucho in the film The Four Horsemen of the Apocalypse *(1921).*

Charlie Chaplin with four-year-old Jackie Coogan on the set for The Kid.

Charlie Chaplin. (1889-1977)

By 1921, Charlie Chaplin was so famous, he was able to travel through Europe without a passport because his face was recognized everywhere, and for good reason. Chaplin had a genius for comedy. As a director and producer, he was a master of details who was able to visualize exactly the effect he wanted and then achieve it. As an actor, he was able to convey a world of emotions with just a small movement, a marked contrast to the flailing arms and sweeping gestures that were still the technique of many silent stars.

Chaplin was born in London and grew up in poverty. From that experience he developed an affection and empathy for the downtrodden "tramps" of the world that was a running theme throughout his film career. In an era when high society was worshiped, Chaplin was one of the few artists to poke fun at the pompous manners of the upper class. In 1925, he released *The Gold Rush*, which hilariously mocked the money-crazed mood of the nation. But social commentary aside, *The Gold Rush* shows why Chaplin was loved by millions. In one memorable scene, Chaplin's character is eagerly expecting the arrival of his ladylove, for whom he has prepared dinner. He pokes two forks in a pair of rolls and performs a little dance of joy with them on the table.

Chaplin's turbulent personal life provided plenty of material for the gossip tabloids in the twenties. During those ten years, he was divorced, then engaged, then broke off the engagement, and then married a different woman, who left him two years later.

When sound movies arrived on the scene, Chaplin predicted that they were a passing fad, no doubt wishing it to be true. As it became increasingly obvious that they were here to stay, Chaplin began to worry about the future of his career: "Occasionally I mused over the possibility of making a sound film, but the thought sickened me, for I realized I could never achieve the excellence of my silent pictures."

Valentino's manager and the undertaker's press agent, a frenzied crowd stretched for eleven blocks outside the funeral home.

Excess was the name of the game when it came to movies. The look of the films became more slick, with elaborate costumes and stage sets. The stars' salaries grew outrageously high. But the most impressive outgrowth of this boom in the movie industry was the theaters it produced. Sometimes accommodating thousands of people, these dream palaces, as they were called, featured uniformed ushers, upholstered seats, and breathtaking chandeliers. Even in smaller towns, the new movie theater was often the most impressive building on Main Street.

And what was showing in these new theaters? The most popular movies were shoot-'em-up Westerns and light-hearted comedies. The silent screen gave rise to comedy geniuses Charlie Chaplin, Harold Lloyd, and Buster Keaton, whose large eyes, deadpan expressions, and incredible physical stunts kept audiences roaring with laughter.

Around the mid-1920s, a new type of motion picture began attracting great crowds, as well as controversy. With titles such as *Sinners in Silk*, and *Forbidden Fruit*, these risqué films mirrored the changing morals and manners of the time. A typical movie ad promised "beautiful jazz babies, champagne baths, midnight revels, petting parties in the purple dawn . . . ." As might be expected from such a description, the plots were weak, and style took precedence over substance. But style was a big seller in the twenties. Middle-class audiences loved studying the manners of the high society characters in the movies. While real life members of the upper class turned up their noses at the films, moviegoers couldn't get enough.

Though the technology for making sound movies was available in 1921, the Hollywood studios were afraid of how audiences might react and so continued to produce silents for several years. But by the end of the twenties, moviegoers seemed to be growing restless and ready for something new. Warner Brothers gave it to them when the first feature length talkie premiered on October 6, 1927. *The Jazz Singer* featured the voice of "The World's Greatest Entertainer," as Al Jolson liked to call himself. In a sign of the times, Jolson played a singer-comedian who performs in blackface. Though the story dripped with sentimentality,

the first sound movie was a smash hit.

At first, talkies were dismissed as a fad that would pass with time, but soon it became clear that there was no going back. Hollywood studios rushed to buy the necessary equipment and soundproof their sets. Many actors who were huge stars of the silent screen, such as Douglas Fairbanks, saw their careers destroyed by the onslaught of talkies. They were casualties in a movie revolution.

The Warners' Theatre proudly advertises the first feature length talkie — Al Jolson in the 1927 movie, The Jazz Singer.

The radio came into its own during the 1920s as every family rushed to buy one. Here a family and friends listen to their new radio with a loudspeaker enabling them all to hear the news, music, and radio shows.

The Rise of Radio

The American public took little interest in radio at first, but once it caught on, the makers of radio sets and parts could barely keep up with public demand. The first radio listeners were electrically minded hobbyists who put together their own amateur wireless sets. They listened to sports scores and music from Victrola records broadcast by amateur stations. In 1920, KDKA in Pittsburgh became the first professional broadcasting station. Soon the fever spread. Newspapers began printing radio sections with diagrams for building receiving sets, and people lined up at hardware stores to buy the necessary parts.

At the beginning of 1922, there were four licensed radio stations. By the end of that year, there were 576. Though not all of those stations survived the next year, the public's interest continued to climb. Sales of radio sets and parts rose from $60,000,000 in 1922 to $842,548,000 in 1929. Soon, receivers were sold already assembled, and earphones were replaced with loudspeakers so a roomful of people could listen together.

With radio, the people in the Midwest could listen to a concert in Boston, a preacher in California, or President Coolidge in the White House, all from the comfort of their own living rooms. Like the automobile, radio had the effect of making the country seem smaller as different regions became less and less isolated from each other.

As radio stations rushed to fill the air waves, they drafted talent wherever they could find it. The most famous announcer of the twenties, Graham McNamee, landed his job after visiting a radio station while on break from jury duty. The station manager was so impressed with McNamee's resonant voice that he gave him a job on the spot.

One of the most popular radio shows ever aired was launched in 1928, and it remains a controversial part of radio history. "Amos 'n' Andy" was a comedy starring two black characters from the south side of Chicago played by white actors. Amos was happy and simple-minded while Andy was lazy and domineering. They were both loved by a huge following of listeners, including President Coolidge. The fact that a show based on racial stereotypes could become the most popular radio program says a great deal about race relations in the twenties. Perhaps as audiences roared with laughter at the wild antics of Amos and Andy, they found it easier to believe that life in the ghetto wasn't really so bad.

A Little Reading Material

Movies and radio were not the only media attracting mass audiences. During the twenties, more and more magazines were reaching circulations of over a million. *Reader's Digest*, *Time*, and the *New Yorker* were born. Instead of relying on mother's advice, young housewives increasingly turned to *Good Housekeeping* and *Ladies Home Journal* for ideas, and the advertisements in such magazines set the standards for the middle-class lifestyle that readers aspired to attain.

But Americans didn't only turn to magazines for new recipes or the latest trends in furniture. Sex and confession magazines with titles such as *True Story*, *True Romance*, and *True Confession* became hugely popular, though they had little to do with the truth. In them, readers found a genre called "sex adventures," which usually told of a girl or boy gone wrong, and the disastrous results of their missteps. Of course, it wasn't the moral of the

A color fashion page from a typical women's magazine of the twenties.

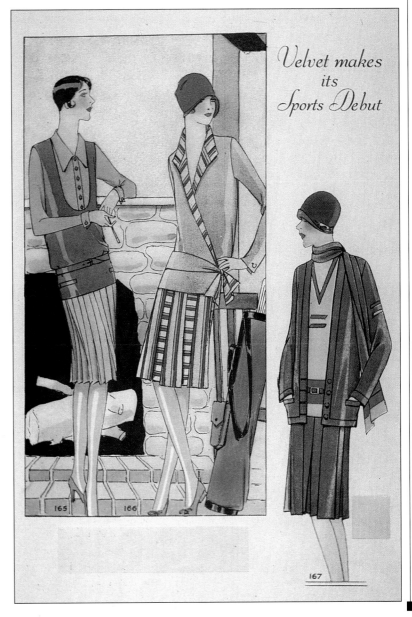

Velvet makes its Sports Debut

"I'll give you a definite maybe."

"A verbal contract isn't worth the paper it's written on."

Movie mogul Samuel Goldwyn

story that readers were interested in but the titillating descriptions of wrongdoing. Typical titles included "What I Told My Daughter the Night Before Her Marriage," and "The Primitive Lover (She wanted a caveman husband)."

Along the same line, tabloid newspapers, which featured smaller pages, large type, and sensational stories, were doing a booming business. The favorite subject of tabloids was crime, surpassed only by sex crimes. Reporters typically didn't let the facts get in the way of a good story. One technique used by tabloids was the composite photograph, which placed famous faces on other people's bodies. In one, the late Rudolph Valentino was shown being greeted at the pearly gates of Heaven by deceased opera singer Enrico Caruso.

As circulation wars developed, other newspapers began following the tabloids' lead. Media hype ran rampant. Any story that had the

makings for popular interest was covered inside out, and it seemed that the entire nation followed along, drawn in by gripping headlines. In 1925, a Kentucky man named Floyd Collins was exploring a cave when a portion of it collapsed, leaving him trapped. An opportunistic reporter crawled in the cave to interview Collins and reported on the rescue attempts with vivid detail. Soon other reporters converged on the scene. For over two weeks, the whole country followed the story as if it involved a personal friend. Collins died before he could be rescued.

The nation also followed with horrified fascination the details of the Leopold and Loeb case. On May 21, 1924, Richard Loeb and Nathan Leopold, Jr., two wealthy, highly intelligent teenagers from Chicago, kidnapped and murdered fourteen-year-old Bobby Franks. In court, they calmly admitted that their

Nathan Leopold, Jr. and Richard Loeb, confessed murderers of Robert Franks. They were sentenced to life imprisonment, escaping the death penalty through the efforts of their lawyer Clarence Darrow, who invoked the theories of Sigmund Freud in their defense.

motive was not the ransom money but the thrill of committing the perfect crime.

The Teapot Dome scandal of the Harding administration was hard-pressed to compete with the love triangles, murders, and other sensational stories that spread across headlines. But by the end of the twenties, many Americans were starting to get that sick feeling that comes from over-indulgence in junk food. In May 1927, the publicity machine served up something different.

Lucky Lindy

By 1927, there had already been several flights across the Atlantic Ocean, mostly over the narrow northern region. But no one had flown between New York and Paris, which was the requirement for the $25,000 prize being offered by hotelier Raymond Orteig.

Two men were killed attempting the flight in the fall of 1926, and four more pilots died trying in the spring of 1927. Even the famous Lieutenant-Commander Richard Byrd, who had flown over the North Pole, cracked up his plane and was injured trying to fly to Paris. Most of the attempts at the $25,000 prize involved well-known pilots and large airplanes, financed with big money. But there was one notable exception. Charles Lindbergh arrived in New York with a small, lightweight plane and plans to fly to Paris alone. He was twenty-five-years-old, shy, tall, and handsome, with a boyish grin. The press instantly pounced on him as the romantic dark horse.

For one week, he prepared his plane for the flight and waited, along with two competitors, for the right weather for taking off. Meanwhile, the press hounded him endlessly. After taking his plane, the *Spirit of St. Louis*, up for a test flight, he damaged the aircraft upon landing while trying to avoid a photographer on the runway. The incident angered Lindbergh, but a newspaper report the next day described him hopping out of the cockpit and saying, "Boys, she's ready and rarin' to go!" To the disciplined young pilot who depended upon accuracy when flying, this type of embellishment of facts was infuriating.

By the time Lindbergh took off on May 20, the entire nation had pinned their hopes on him. The next day, reports came in of his plane being sighted over Ireland and then England. When he reached Paris, a huge crowd of ecstatic people rushed his plane. Before returning home, Lindbergh was decorated with awards in France, Belgium, and Britain. He received them all with sincere modesty, and Americans couldn't have been prouder. The *Philadelphia Inquirer* proclaimed: "Lindbergh personifies America . . . every parent sees him as an ideal son."

In New York, he received a hero's welcome including a ticker tape parade that rivalled the celebrations at the end of World War I. Among the many honors heaped upon Lindbergh, including the Distinguished Flying Cross and the Congressional Medal of Honor, a town in Texas was named after him. Newspapers printed portraits of him "suitable for framing." And that's just what people did. Soon Lindbergh's face appeared in schoolrooms, railroad stations, restaurants, and homes throughout the country. After years of government corruption, sex scandals, and murder trials, Lindbergh's combination of

"Do you think you can cure the hatred and maladjustments of the world by hanging them? You simply show your ignorance and your hate when you say it. You may heal and cure hatred with love and understanding, but you can only add fuel to the flames with cruelty and hating."

Clarence Darrow, arguing against the death penalty at the trial of Leopold and Loeb

Charles Lindbergh. (1902-1974)

A former stunt pilot, Charles Lindbergh was working for the airmail service when he decided that he could fly from New York to Paris. Like everyone else, he had followed the failed attempts of other pilots to make the flight, but he believed he knew the solution — a single-engine plane flown solo. And he felt confident that he could do it. After all, he was used to flying alone on his airmail route between St. Louis and Chicago, carrying heavy loads and staying awake for up to forty hours at a time.

When the unknown young pilot first announced his plans, he received little attention. But when Lindbergh flew his specially built *Spirit of St. Louis* by himself nonstop from California to New York in record time, he suddenly stepped into the limelight.

On the rainy morning of May 20, 1927, after a sleepless night, Lindbergh asked himself if he would fly his airmail plane in such weather. His answer was yes. And so, with a bag of sandwiches and a thermos of water, he took off for a thirty-six hundred mile flight.

Lindbergh was an extremely disciplined and detail-oriented pilot. He had considered every ounce of material to be carried on the flight, foregoing even a parachute because he considered its extra weight unjustified. As he flew for hour after hour through the fog, Lindbergh was thankful that the little plane was so unstable, for its jolts and swerves helped him stay alert. Still, he found himself fighting to stay awake and slipped into a semiconsciousness at times, seeing and hearing hallucinations.

Finally, after over thirty-three hours of flying, Lindbergh spotted Paris. He circled the dimly lit runway and landed, hoping to find someone who spoke a little English and a place to spend the night. He was totally unprepared for the swarms of people who broke through metal fences and police guards to greet his plane. No sooner had he landed than souvenir hunters were tearing at the *Spirit of St. Louis.* When Lindbergh attempted to leave the plane, he was lifted over the mob's heads and carried along. "It was like drowning in a human sea," he remembered later.

At last, Lindbergh was whisked away to safety. After sixty-three hours, he had finally found restful sleep. He would need it. For when Lindbergh awoke, he was the greatest hero of the western world.

modesty and daring individuality were like a breath of fresh air, and the American public breathed him in deeply.

The Golden Age of Sports

Another rich source of heroes for the twenties was the world of sports. Americans in search of excitement were flocking like never before to baseball diamonds, football stadiums, and ringside seats, as sports became a national mania.

In 1919, nine White Sox players were blacklisted for throwing the World Series in what came to be known as the Black Sox Scandal. But before baseball fans had a chance to become too disillusioned with the game, Babe Ruth came along and began breaking records. In 1919, he surpassed the long-standing home run record of twenty-seven by two runs. But that was nothing. In 1921, he hit fifty-nine home runs, living up to his nickname, the Sultan of Swat. Soon baseball fans were breaking records of their own as attendance in the stands doubled figures from prewar years. Everyone wanted to see the Babe, or the home team equivalent, hit one out of the park.

Women athletes also achieved hero status as they made exciting breakthroughs in the world of sports. In 1926, a nineteen-year-old Olympic swimmer named Gertrude Ederle astonished the world by not only becoming the first woman to swim the English Channel, but by doing it faster than any of the five men who had completed the treacherous, thirty-mile course.

College football became incredibly popular in the twenties and, by the time of the Depression, was grossing over $21 million annually. This was due in large part to the fact that college enrollment more than doubled during the decade. As universities

Babe Ruth. (1895-1948)

Born in a rough neighborhood of Baltimore, George Ruth already had a police record at the age of seven when he entered St. Mary's Industrial School, a combination orphanage and reform institution. It was there that he learned to play the game of baseball.

Nicknamed "Babe" as a rookie in the major leagues, Ruth started out as a pitcher and a good one at that. But with a bat, he was more than good. He was amazing. During spring training in 1919, Ruth smashed a ball 597 feet. It was the first in a long stream of hitting records. No matter what strategy pitchers used, Ruth's bat managed to find the ball, and one of his teammates suggested that the best strategy was "Pitch and duck."

With his skinny legs, barrel-shaped body, and broad, homely features, he was hardly the most handsome of sports heroes, but he was certainly the best-loved. The crowds of fans eager to see Ruth play were so huge that Yankee Stadium was built to accommodate them in 1923. It's still known as "the house that Ruth built."

Before Ruth's time, most runs were scored through a succession of singles, and games usually ended with low scores. But then a new manufacturing process made baseballs more likely to be hit farther, and spitballs were banned. Ruth's slugfests signified a transformation of the game. Though baseball purists complained that skill was being replaced with brute strength, the fans didn't seem to mind.

In many ways, the Babe's nickname fit his personality. His temper often landed him in trouble, and with his enormous salary, he was like a kid in a candy store. Ruth was fond of fast cars and flashy women. He liked his reputation as a glutton and did what he could to keep it up. During the course of an evening out with friends, Ruth consumed four porterhouse steaks, eight hot dogs, four pieces of apple pie á la mode, eight bottles of Coca-Cola, and a few side orders of fries and salad. But no matter how wild a night he'd had, Ruth always showed up at the ball park ready to play. Biographer Marshall Smelzer described Babe Ruth as "the idol of everybody who would like to flout every rule of conduct and still be a champion."

(Right) Dempsey blasts Luis Firpo out of the ring in this 1924 painting by George Bellows.

Jack Dempsey. (1895-1983)

Jack Dempsey was born in a small Colorado town to a pioneer family who had arrived there in a covered wagon. Although he made his living for a time as a miner, his dream was to be a prizefighter. He soaked his face in brine to make it as tough as leather and chewed pine gum straight from the trees to strengthen his jaw. Eventually, the young boxer hooked up with promoter Tex Rickard, who arranged for him to fight the heavyweight champion of the world, Jess Willard, on July 4, 1919. Up until this point, boxing had been considered a marginal sport, played in sleazy arenas attended by thugs and lowlifes. But Rickard changed that. With the Dempsey-Willard fight, he brought boxing into respectable stadiums and made it attractive to the middle and upper classes. Soon the likes of John D. Rockefeller were snapping up ringside seats and inviting Dempsey to their social events.

When Dempsey took the title from Willard, he achieved instant fame and fortune. A Hollywood studio even offered him a role as "Daredevil Jack" in an action serial. As he freely admitted, Dempsey was not much of an actor, but to make matters worse, he couldn't quite get the hang of pulling his punches and kept knocking his fellow actors out cold.

The new champion didn't bask in the public's adoration for long. A false rumor was spread that Dempsey was a draft dodger, and in the hyper-patriotic atmosphere of 1920, rumor was as good as fact for many. Dempsey never completely shook the story.

Ironically, Dempsey regained his popularity after losing the title to Gene Tunney in 1926. As a boxer and as a man, Tunney was the complete opposite of Dempsey. While Dempsey was equipped with a brutally powerful punch, Tunney had technique. And while Dempsey was a rough-edged man, shaped by the frontier, Tunney quoted Shakespeare and displayed an arrogant attitude. Soon fans and sportswriters missed the modesty and earthiness of the former heavyweight champion of the world, Jack Dempsey.

began realizing the enormous sums of money to be made on football, a wave of stadium construction began. Perhaps the most exciting player of the era was Harold "Red" Grange, playing for the University of Illinois. His amazing feats on the field catapulted him into such fame that he even signed a movie contract, though his acting career was far less impressive.

The enormous popularity of boxing in the twenties also helped push sports into the realm of big business. In 1921, Jack Dempsey defended his title against George Carpentier in the first of several million-dollar fights during the decade. In an article describing the fight, H.L. Mencken wrote, "Dempsey has a wallop in his right hand like the collision of a meteorite with the Alps." But perhaps the most famous fight of the twenties was Dempsey's attempt to win back his title from Gene Tunney. In the seventh round, Dempsey knocked Tunney out, but the referee refused to start the count until Dempsey retreated to a neutral corner, which took five seconds. The count finally began, and on number eight, Tunney stood up. He went on to win the fight. Five boxing fans reportedly died of heart failure listening to the bout on the radio.

Tennis, which had been considered a game for phony snobs, became a

New Yorker Gertrude Ederle was the first woman to swim the English Channel. The nineteen-year-old completed the crossing in record time — fourteen hours, thirty-one minutes. "It had to be done and I did it," she remarked. Later Ederle tragically lost her hearing as a result of her swim.

favorite sport with the help of Bill Tilden, who won at Wimbeldon in 1920 and continued to dominate the sport for most of the decade. Golfer Bobby Jones seemed unbeatable after winning the U.S. Open in 1923, and fans were awed by his near-perfect technique.

But Americans were not satisfied to be mere spectators. More and more people were taking up sports themselves as Victorian standards of propriety that had restricted clothing and activities faded away. Tennis was one of the most popular choices, but golf experienced a phenomenal growth. In 1920, there were less than two thousand golf courses in the United States. By 1930, that number had more than tripled. Businessmen took to negotiating deals in knickers and checkered socks while playing a leisurely eighteen holes.

The image of the twenties as one long party is no doubt based in part on the nonstop stream of fads that came and went during the decade. The latest song, dance, style, or game spread through the country like wildfire, and when the novelty wore off, a new fad stepped in to take its place. Radios, movies, newsreels, and newspapers did their part to spread the latest sensations, allowing radio listeners in Seattle to tire of the song, "Yes, We Have No Bananas" at just about the same time that Chicago listeners did.

The Chinese game of Mah Jong was all the rage in 1923, and just about anyone with two good legs learned to dance the Charleston. Perhaps the silliest fad of the twenties was flagpole sitting, the champion of which was Alvin "Shipwreck" Kelly, who perched atop a flagpole in Baltimore for twenty-three days and seven hours. Mothers worried about the dangers of dance marathons,

The craziest 1920s fad of them all — Alvin "Shipwreck" Kelly atop a flagpole in Union City, New Jersey, in 1929 at the start of another record-breaking attempt.

where young couples clung to one another in complete exhaustion, dancing for days at a time in pursuit of first prize.

One of the most popular fads of the twenties proved to have staying power, though the initial frenzy that greeted it eventually died down. In 1925, Richard Simon and his friend Max Schuster launched a new publishing company with *The Crossword Puzzle Book*. Though crosswords had been around for over ten years, this was the first time they were collected in a book. It became an instant bestseller and started the latest national mania. Soon millions of Americans from all walks of life were obsessed with filling in the little boxes of their puzzles. In Chicago, a woman took her husband to court, claiming that he was ruining their marriage by spending all of his free time working crossword puzzles. The judge put a limit of three puzzles a day on the husband.

CHAPTER 7
Changing Morals and Manners

The Rise of the Moderns

While the Communist Revolution was underway in Russia, a much more subtle erosion of the old order was taking place in the United States. The Victorian manners and Puritan morals that had governed society for so long were being cast aside in favor of all that was considered modern. No blood was spilled, but battle lines were drawn as defenders of the old order fought against what they considered an assault on all that was proper, decent, and holy. Taboos fell by the wayside. Women were exposing previously hidden parts of their bodies, such as

Fanny Brice (seated on the piano) prepares for a radio broadcast from the Hotel Astor in New York City. Note the two characters in blackface, still an acceptable form of entertainment in the twenties. At the piano is Paul Whiteman.

Fanny Brice. (1891-1951)

A self-confessed ham, Fanny Brice worked her way up in the theater with a combination of natural talent and hungry ambition. By 1920, she was a favorite star of the legendary Ziegfeld Follies and a vaudeville sensation. With her wide smile, large nose, and expressive eyebrows, Brice made audiences laugh so hard that she "laid 'em out in the rows," as she put it. She could mimic any accent, and in some of her most hilarious skits, she satirized doting Jewish mothers in Yiddish dialect. But she was also a powerful torch singer who poured her heart into moving lyrics about love gone wrong.

Off stage, Brice was a combination of high-class elegance and down-to-earth bawdiness. She loved to surround herself with the finer things in life and was always impeccably dressed. Her children called her Mademoiselle. But she also was fond of four-letter words and had absolutely no time for snobbery. She called everyone "Kid."

In 1919, Brice married a handsome, sophisticated swindler named Nick Arnstein, who spent the better part of their marriage either running from the law, facing trial, or in prison. At one point, Fanny was forced to turn to gangster Arnold Rothstein, the mastermind behind the Black Sox scandal, for money to bail Arnstein out of jail. Though Fanny was devoted to Arnstein, she finally realized that she would never change him and sought a divorce.

In the late twenties, Fanny married songwriter and speakeasy owner Billy Rose, who wrote "Paper Moon," "Me and My Shadow," and other popular songs. Four inches shorter and eight years younger than Brice, Rose was the complete opposite of Arnstein. With their combined talents, her career reached new heights. Fanny Brice's climb to fame and rocky personal life were immortalized by the movie *Funny Girl*, in which she was played by Barbara Streisand.

shoulders, throats, and even knees; some people actually began discussing sex openly and in public; religion seemed to be losing ground; and parents worried that their teenage children were becoming increasingly restless and difficult to control.

What gave rise to this rebellion? Obviously, it was not an organized revolution that was launched overnight. Some changes that had begun before the war were sped up as an effect of that catastrophic world event. The war itself exposed millions of men and women to unprecedented horrors that caused them to reexamine what they had blindly accepted as truth. It also exposed young soldiers and nurses overseas to "continental" ways and manners, the effects of which are hinted at in the popular postwar song, "How You Gonna Keep 'Em Down on the Farm After They've Seen Paree?" Some parents blamed the auto for their troubles, as it gave youngsters the freedom to drive away from the bosom of their family in search of a good time. The good people of Middle America wondered if movies and radio weren't eroding family ties as they replaced singing, neighborhood small talk, and other forms of make-your-own fun. As if these lifestyle changes and postwar side effects weren't enough, advances in science and psychology shook the foundations of centuries-old belief systems.

All of these factors made for an exciting, confusing, exhilarating, and, to some people, frightening period of change in the United States.

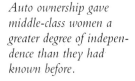

Auto ownership gave middle-class women a greater degree of independence than they had known before.

"[There has been] a change for the worse during the past year in feminine dress, dancing, manners and general moral standards."

Pittsburgh Observer

With their drop waists and short skirts, the fashions of these 1928 women were radically different from the long skirts and tight corsets worn by their mothers at the same age.

The Changing American Woman

As the "fairer sex," women were expected to uphold the morals and manners of society. But the new American woman was changing her ideas of what was considered proper. A comparison of popular fashions in 1915 to those of 1925 provides visible evidence of this change. In prewar years, women wore high, lace-up boots, and hemlines were at the ankle or lower, where it seemed they'd been forever. Most women had long hair, and the emphasis in fashion was on the shapeliness of the feminine body. Under their dresses, women wore layer upon layer of cotton underclothes and a restraining corset that could make breathing,

While men continued to believe in women as "the weaker sex" for years after women won the vote, individual women, like Nellie Ross, governor of Wyoming from 1924-28, proved they could be just as capable as men in public office.

much less bending over, a difficult activity. Despite how uncomfortable they were, author Ben Hecht remembered that in 1912, women were arrested for going shopping without their corsets on.

Ten years later, women were wearing low-cut pumps, and hemlines had risen almost all the way to the knee. Underclothes usually consisted of a single layer of silk. Corsets were mercifully becoming a thing of the past, and gone too were the accentuated curves of the female silhouette. Instead, most dresses featured a dropped waist or no waist at all, giving the wearer's figure a boyish look. The new hairstyles added to the effect as more and more women had their hair bobbed, or cut short.

As these boyish, less restraining fashion trends indicate, women were becoming more independent and assertive. During the war, many women took jobs, and a large portion of them kept those jobs even after the soldiers came home. For working-class women, however, a job was a necessity rather than a career choice, for even during Coolidge Prosperity, many families required two incomes. As time-saving appliances, canned goods, and bakeries became more common, women were tied less to the house. The auto also gave them more freedom.

Feminism After the Vote

The Nineteenth Amendment, which granted women the right to vote in 1920, fundamentally changed women's status in the United States. But the political role that women played for the rest of the decade did not live up to the expectations of the suffragettes, who had predicted that the nation would be transformed by women voters unwilling to put up with business as usual. Women, they argued, would demand reform and insist that a greater emphasis be placed on social causes such as education and poverty. As a result, the country would become a better, more just place to live.

Perhaps such idealistic goals are the fuel that keeps political activists going. In reality, not only did these dramatic transformations not happen,

but many women did not even exercise their newly won right. And most of those who made it to the polls voted the way their husbands or fathers did. Although the vote could be granted with the stroke of a pen, the social role of women took much, much longer to change. After being expected for so many years to follow the lead of the men in their lives, most women were not inclined to cast a dissenting vote. The idealistic suffragettes were also naive to predict that all women would vote as a bloc for social reform and economic justice, for women were just as likely as men to have differing political views based on their social and economic backgrounds.

Nevertheless, women's lobbying groups did become a force in Washington, and among their accomplishments was the 1924 Child Labor Amendment to the Constitution. A number of women were also sent to serve in Congress, though two-thirds of them arrived there to fill out the terms of their deceased husbands, and most of them were not reelected. One of the most distinguished of the first women legislators was Nellie Ross, governor of Wyoming from 1924 to 1928, who proved that women could serve with

Women went out to work as a necessity during World War I and continued to swell the ranks of white collar workers during the twenties. By 1930, 736,000 women worked as clerks, wrappers, cashiers, or, like these 1926 A T & T employees, switchboard operators. Typically, women's jobs did not command high wages and offered few opportunities for advancement.

Amelia Earhart (1898-1937?)

As a young woman, Amelia Earhart was intense and restless. She knew that she wanted to do something important with her life, but didn't know what it should be. The answer became clear to her after her first airplane ride. " 'I think I'd like to fly,' I told my family casually that evening, knowing full well I'd die if I didn't," she recalled.

Earhart scraped together money to take lessons whenever she could, but she soon found how difficult it was for a woman to make a living by flying. She was occupied as a social worker in April 1928 when she received a call from a publicity man asking if she would be willing to ride in an airplane across the Atlantic. Charles Lindbergh's transatlantic flight had spawned a flurry of copycats seeking similar fame and fortune. Fourteen people had died trying, including three women.

The terms of the flight were that the pilot and mechanic, both men, would be paid handsomely, but Earhart would receive nothing for risking her life except the opportunity to advance her career in aviation. She quickly accepted. Though Earhart hoped to do some of the flying herself, she was never given the chance during the entire twenty-hour and forty-minute trip. After arriving in Wales, she privately complained, "I was just baggage." But to the press she expressed enthusiasm and gave the pilot (whom she had discovered was an alcoholic) all the credit.

The American public hailed Earhart as a heroine for being the first woman to cross the Atlantic in an airplane, and the press soon dubbed her "Lady Lindy." Though Earhart was shy by nature and uncomfortable as the object of public adoration, she was eager to use the opportunity that her fame gave her to promote commercial aviation and women pilots. She flew around the country giving lectures to packed crowds.

In following years, eager to justify her fame as a woman pilot rather than as a passenger, Earhart would set a multitude of flight records. It was while pursuing her most ambitious goal, a flight around the world, that her airplane disappeared. The disappearance and probable demise of Earhart remains a compelling mystery today.

as much efficiency and decisiveness as men. This was no small feat, considering the prejudice facing women in the twenties. In a 1928 article in *Harper's*, the author declared, "The reason that women are more subject to hysteria than men is in plain terms that their brains are weaker, more easily unbalanced."

Without the vote as a mission to rally around, a split developed within the feminist movement after 1920. One of the divisive issues raised was the Equal Rights Amendment, which many feminists feared would threaten the special legislation they had pushed for to protect women, such as maternity insurance. Another rift developed over the future of the feminist movement. Some, including feminist leader Carrie Chapman Catt, believed that integration into the current process was the key to empowerment, and that women needed to learn to play the game as well as men to make advances in business, politics, and other areas. Activist Jane Addams was among those in the opposing camp who believed that by operating as a separate, unified interest group, women would have more influence and a louder voice.

Meanwhile, in addition to the divisions from within, feminism was suffering from something of an image problem. In an era when, on the one hand, carefree youthfulness was the ideal and, on the other hand, a conservative political atmosphere prevailed, feminism seemed to strike out on both

counts. Feminists were stereotyped as frumpy, humorless radicals. Even the famous aviator Amelia Earhart seemed aware of this image when she described her feminist leanings while denying the label in a letter to a friend. "I cannot claim to be a feminist," she wrote, "but do rather enjoy seeing women tackling all kinds of new problems — new for them, that is."

The Fabulous Flappers

While the various feminist groups devised strategies for changing social conditions, an army of carefree flappers was stomping all over social

The daring, new one-piece bathing suits on display at the 1923 Atlantic City beauty pageant.

CULTURE AND SOCIETY

For further information see primary source entries on pages

11: 1469-70, 1509-10, 1516-18, 1520;
12: 1613-17, 1671-73, 1719-21

customs. Young, self-confident, assertive, and independent, the typical flapper cared more about parties than politics, but she played an important part in changing attitudes toward women nonetheless. Some say they were named flappers because they were like young birds attempting to fly before their wings were fully developed, while others say the name came from the sound their unfastened galoshes made when they walked. In any case, they are an indelible image of the twenties, with their beaded dresses, long necklaces, and stockings rolled down to just above the knees.

Much to the horror of their parents, young flappers went against all the prescribed rules of ladylike conduct. They smoked, drank, danced wildly, and gave out kisses freely. Some believed that, by speaking frankly and asserting their sexual freedom, this new breed of woman was breaking down barriers. But most flappers were not really concerned with equality for women. They were more interested in catching a man.

Zelda Fitzgerald, writer and wife of novelist F. Scott Fitzgerald, wrote of the flapper, "She flirted because it was fun to flirt and wore a one-piece bathing suit because she had a good figure, she covered her face with paint and powder because she didn't need it and she refused to be bored chiefly because she wasn't boring. She was conscious that the things she did were the things she had always wanted to do."

Apparently, one of the things she had always wanted to do was to wear make-up. Before the war, ruby red lips and painted eyebrows were worn only by "loose women," but in the twenties, cosmetics became a booming business, and beauty parlors sprang up throughout the country. Beauty contests were another product of the twenties, featuring male judges whose job it was to size up young women wearing the shocking new one-piece bathing suits that would have gotten them arrested a few years earlier.

The Impact of Psychology

Accused of having loose morals and behaving in an unladylike manner, a sophisticated flapper might respond with a minilecture on Freud, explaining that repressing one's desires was unhealthy. During the twenties, Freud's theories, or at least popular interpretations of them, came into vogue among the moderns. Though he had lectured in the United States over a decade earlier, the public didn't embrace his ideas until after the war, when the younger generation was seeking to break from the past. They referred to Freud to explain that Puritan ideas of sin were responsible for just about everything that was wrong with society. If only everyone could undergo psychoanalysis (Freud's psychiatric therapy which uses free association, dream therapy and other techniques to explore repressed or unconscious conflicts and anxieties), they believed, the world would be cured of all its ills. In the meantime, society could be made healthier by bringing sex out into the open. Soon sex was a popular topic of conversation that supposedly shocked only unsophisticated people.

Sexual freedom was not only talked about but acted upon as

well. The young generation of the twenties was far more likely than their parents to be sexually experienced before they were married. Of course, the popularity of Freudianism was not the only cause for this sexual revolution. Though it was illegal to dispense birth control information and devices (except by doctors, and even then only to prevent disease), they were still more available than ever before, thanks in part to crusaders such as Margaret Sanger. As the fear of becoming pregnant was eased and women were growing increasingly independent, they were more likely to become sexually active without entering into matrimony.

Behaviorism was another school of psychology that spread through the country in the twenties. Promoted by Dr. John B. Watson, behaviorism seemed to fit in with the rapid industrialization taking place, as it explained that man was like a machine. He could be programmed to behave in any number of ways through mental and physical stimuli. In the face of such scientific postulations, old ideas about morals and manners seemed somehow shaky and even irrelevant.

One of the trendier, quick-fix psychological ideas to catch on came from a French pharmacist named Emile Coue. He travelled through the country explaining to eager audiences that they could change their lives by repeating twenty times, in the morning and evening: "Day by day, in every way, I am getting better and better." The power of "positive thinking" was certainly becoming extremely popular — placing blame for failure squarely on the individual.

Science versus Religion

One of the main reasons that psychology had such an impact in the twenties, aside from the fact that it offered convenient justifications for breaking the old rules, was that it was a science, and anything scientific had

The psychologist Sigmund Freud, whose theories influenced many young people in the 1920s. Mostly they wanted some scientific excuse for pursuing their liberated beliefs in free love and wild behavior.

instant authority. As tremendous advances were being made in medicine and technology, the public began to believe that perhaps science held the answers to all of the world's problems. Newspapers began devoting sections to science news, and though most readers couldn't really understand Albert Einstein's theory of relativity, they knew it was important.

Just as modern psychological theories conflicted with Victorian and Puritan codes of conduct, the theory of evolution ran head-on into the fundamentalist doctrine of creationism. The country's attention was

"When motherhood becomes the fruit of a deep yearning, not the result of ignorance or accident, its children will become the foundation of a new race."

Margaret Sanger,
Women and the New Race, 1920

"Mother bore eleven children; she died at forty-eight. My father died at eighty."

Margaret Sanger

Margaret Sanger. (1883-1966)

Margaret Sanger was the middle child in a large, poor family. As a nurse in the immigrant slums of New York City, she saw many desperate women burdened with too many mouths to feed and too little to feed them. Outraged at the bleak conditions she had witnessed and experienced, Sanger joined forces with radical groups seeking change in the idealistic prewar years.

Eventually, she decided to concentrate her activism on promoting birth control as a cure to the social ills that so disturbed her. Sanger believed that as long as the lower class continued to have large families, business would be able to take advantage of workers because there would never be a shortage of people to fill a job, no matter how miserable it was. She promoted birth control as a means to economic justice, as well as increased freedom and power for women. Sanger declared, "No woman can call herself free until she can choose consciously whether she will or will not be a mother." A practitioner of "free love" herself, she also promoted birth control as a means by which women could enjoy sex instead of being afraid of its consequences.

Sanger continually challenged the laws against the dissemination of birth control information and devices. As a result, she was jailed several times. In 1921, the first American Birth Control Conference concluded in New York with a public meeting. Before Margaret Sanger could give her prepared speech, the meeting was raided by police, reportedly in response to the urging of Catholic Church officials. The news of the raid caused a public outcry and actually won support for Sanger's cause, though the opposition continued to fight against birth control and censored Sanger whenever they could.

During the twenties, Sanger downplayed her prewar radicalism and enlisted support from socially powerful men and women. In a controversial move, she aligned herself with eugenicists who embraced birth control as a means for improving the human race by cutting down on the reproduction of the "unfit" members of society. A lively, attractive, and idealistic woman, Sanger could also be extremely stubborn and tenacious. To some, she was a dangerous radical; to others, she was a crusader for freedom.

Margaret Sanger (center) with Mrs. Anna Kennedy, the executive secretary of the Birth Control League and Dr. Dorothy Booker, a director of the League.

William Jennings Bryan. (1860-1925)

Hailed as the Great Commoner, William Jennings Bryan was a lifelong champion of the poor and a crusader against the influence of wealth in politics. Bryan was an eloquent speaker with an evangelical style, and for decades, he was one of the most popular lecturers in the country. An unsuccessful candidate for president in 1896, 1900, and 1908, his future rival Clarence Darrow supported him in his last two bids. Though his campaigns failed, he was very influential in the Democratic party, playing a key role in securing the nomination for Wilson. President Wilson rewarded Bryan by appointing him secretary of state.

When the Republicans took over in Washington, Bryan became depressed about the government and turned instead to the "American politics of faith." Always a deeply religious man, Bryan became increasingly fundamentalist as he grew older. He was a man of the nineteenth century, raised in the rural heartland, and as such, he was disturbed by the fast-growing cities populated by a young generation of doubters.

Bryan believed that it was the public schools' duty to provide moral as well as intellectual instruction, but that, in the end, a good heart was more important that a trained mind. Printed copies of his lecture, "Is the Bible True?" were passed among state legislators in Tennessee, most likely helping in the passage of the anti-evolution law there.

For the last eleven years of his life, Bryan suffered from diabetes. Treatment for the illness was still in an experimental stage, and by the time of the Scopes Monkey Trial, Bryan's family noticed that the diabetes was "hurting his ability to remember and speak consistently." It was a sick man who took the witness stand to be questioned by the sharp-tongued Darrow.

After his death, crowds of mostly country people gathered at small depots to pay their respects as his funeral train made its way to Arlington National Cemetery in Washington.

focused on that conflict with what came to be known as the Scopes Monkey Trial of 1925. But before delving into the details of that case, it is important to understand the buildup of the conflict.

As the United States entered the twenties, there was a feeling that religion was losing ground. For one thing, the church had to compete with radios, movies, and Sunday drives for the public's attention. For another, scientific discoveries led some people to believe that the idea of miracles and faith in the unseen was outdated. As a result, a split developed in the Protestant church in 1921. The modernists believed that their religion should be modified to take science into consideration, though some people felt this only further weakened the influence of the church. The fundamentalists took a completely different approach.

They stood by a literal interpretation of the Bible, right down to the creation of Eve from Adam's rib. To them, the Bible, not science, was the ultimate source of truth.

The fundamentalists made their voices heard wherever they could, but especially in the South. In 1924, Baptist legislators in Tennessee pushed through a bill that made it illegal for their public schools "to teach any theory that denies the story of the Divine Creation of man as taught in the Bible, and to teach instead that man has descended from a lower order of animals." The law was quickly brought to the attention of the American Civil Liberties Union, and they began a search for a teacher to serve as a plaintiff in a test case. Twenty-four-year-old John T. Scopes, biology teacher at Central High School in Dayton, Tennessee, was persuaded to let himself be arrested for teaching evolution in the classroom.

The trial instantly became known across the nation, with all the attendant ballyhoo and circus antics. William Jennings Bryan, an

Clarence Darrow. (1857-1938)

The most famous and controversial lawyer of his time, Clarence Darrow fought on the side of the underprivileged and for freedom in all its forms. He was a complex man who was both cynical and sentimental about humankind. Darrow could be melodramatic one moment, then bitterly sarcastic the next. Over six feet tall with broad, stooped shoulders, he typically appeared in court in a wrinkled suit with messy hair, hooking his thumbs in his suspenders or the arm holes of his vest as he argued his case.

As bigotry, censorship, and hate-mongering flared up throughout the twenties, Darrow took on cases that to him symbolized the injustice of society, no matter how unpopular his clients were. During the height of the Red Scare, he defended Communists' right to free speech. In 1924, he took on two of the most unpopular defendants ever, Leopold and Loeb. Though the "millionaire murderers" were hardly underprivileged, Darrow viewed the case as a fight against capital punishment. The sensational press coverage of the case had stirred up a blood lust in the public, and most people expected Leopold and Loeb to be hung. Darrow pleaded for the two men's lives, and Leopold, who had not shed a tear throughout the ordeal, later remembered, "He made even me feel with him that terrific tenderness of his for the whole undeserving human race." The judge sentenced Leopold and Loeb to life in prison.

In 1926, Darrow defended an African-American doctor and ten other black men in a case that involved mob violence that had flared up when the doctor and his family moved to a white neighborhood of Detroit. When a large mob formed outside of the house and began pelting it with rocks, the men inside the house panicked. Shots were fired and a white man was killed. Darrow argued that it was self-defense. In his closing arguments to the jury, he said, "I speak for a million blacks who have some hope and faith remaining in the institutions of this land.... I ask you in the name of the future to do justice in this case." Though the first trial resulted in a hung jury, all eleven men were later acquitted.

old-fashioned fundamentalist and three-time Democratic candidate for president, volunteered his services to the prosecution team. Upon arriving in Dayton, Bryan declared, "The contest between evolution and Christianity is a duel to the death. If evolution wins in Dayton, Christianity goes — not suddenly, of course, but gradually — for the two cannot stand together." Clarence Darrow, liberal trial lawyer and avowed agnostic, joined the ACLU's defense team. Soon the dusty little town of Dayton was swamped with reporters, cameramen, professors, and religious revivalists. Lemonade and hot dog stands did a booming business, and signs urging "SWEETHEARTS, COME TO JESUS" stood nearby booths selling pins that read "YOUR OLD MAN'S A MONKEY." For those who couldn't make it to Dayton, WGN broadcast the trial nationally on radio.

Though the real issue of the case was whether the Tennessee law violated the separation of church and state, Darrow was unsuccessful in having the case moved to a federal court, where Constitutional cases must be tried. Instead, he tried to prove that evolutionism did not necessarily conflict with the Bible. The judge, however, would not allow testimony from the scientists and theologians the defense had brought to Dayton. With the defense's strategy thwarted, a guilty verdict seemed inevitable, and most of the reporters left town in search of a new story. But then, in a dramatic move, Darrow called Bryan to the witness stand to testify as an expert on the Bible. Bryan agreed, eager to defend his faith against a man he had called "the greatest atheist and agnostic in the United States."

Due to the large crowd of observers and the soaring July temperatures, the judge moved the proceedings outdoors to a shady spot under a large tree. Darrow's questioning began calmly, but his tone turned sarcastic as Bryan's answers affirmed his belief in the literal truth of the Bible. At one point, Darrow asked Bryan if he really believed that a "big fish" swallowed Jonah. "Yes, sir," replied Bryan. "Let me add: one miracle is just as easy to believe as another." "It is for you," snapped Darrow. As the questioning proceeded, tempers rose. Bryan complained to the judge, "The only purpose Mr. Darrow has is to slur at the Bible. . . ." Darrow objected, "I am examining you on your fool ideas that no intelligent Christian on earth believes." The judge declared court adjourned and ended the trial the next day. Scopes was quickly found guilty and fined $100. In an appeal to the State Supreme Court, the law forbidding lessons on evolution was upheld, but Scopes's conviction was overturned due to a technicality.

Though the fundamentalists won the case, Darrow had achieved his hoped for effect. Bryan's testimony made him appear ridiculous, ignorant, and outdated. He died one week after the trial ended. On his tombstone are the words, "He Kept the Faith."

The Scopes trial in Tennessee was indicative of a struggle going on throughout the country in the twenties, between those who wished to hold on to the uncomplicated, familiar ideas of the past and those eager to embrace all that was modern.

What's Left for the Moderns?

When the Scopes Monkey Trial ended, most Americans turned their attention to the next tabloid scandal or the latest crazy fad. Busy being good consumers and taking in all that movies, radio, and the auto had to offer, most people didn't spend much time pondering the moral state of the nation.

But to those whose life's work it was to consider such things, to intellectuals, writers, and artists, the question arose, "What now?" As the influence of religion and the Victorian code of conduct were weakening, what, if anything, would take their place? Psychology was urging people to throw off the shackles of guilt and repression, yet freedom could be a very confusing thing. Journalist and author Walter Lippmann described the dilemma facing modern men and women in *A Preface to Morals*, written in 1929: "There are no conventions, no taboos, no gods, priests, princes, fathers, or revelations which they must accept. Yet the result is not so good as they thought it would be. The prison door is wide open. They stagger out into trackless space under a blinding sun. They find it nerve-wracking."

A Charleston dancing contest in 1926. Developed in Charleston, South Carolina, this dance set the pace for the roaring twenties.

CHAPTER 8
Advances in the Arts

An Atmosphere of Stimulation

Amid the exciting environment of the twenties, the arts thrived in the United States. The aftermath of the nation's first involvement in an international war, the amazing march forward of technology, expanding cities, and the revolution in morals and manners all provided ample inspiration. In the past, Europe, especially Britain, had greatly influenced arts in the United States, but as American writers, painters, musicians, and architects interpreted the modern world, an American identity emerged.

The Lost Generation

The turmoil of the twenties produced a wealth of exciting and enduring works of literature that offer insights into the prevailing attitudes of a new

Mr. and Mrs. Chester Dale Dining Out, (c1925) by Guy Pene Dubois, painter of people and fashion.

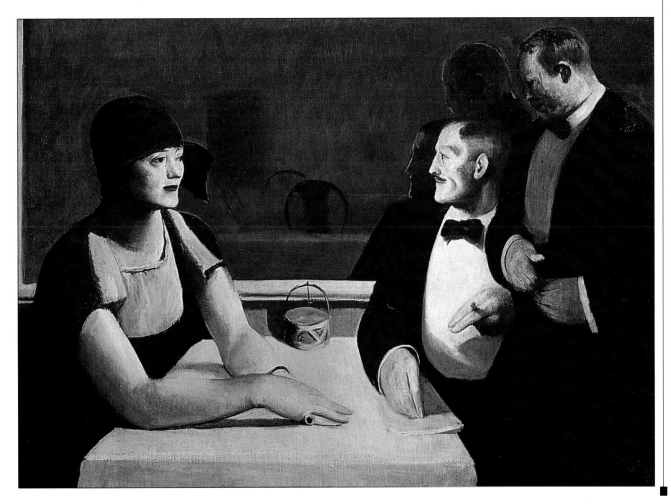

IN THIS TEMPLE
AS IN THE HEARTS OF THE PEOPLE
FOR WHOM HE SAVED THE UNION
THE MEMORY OF ABRAHAM LINCOLN
IS ENSHRINED FOREVER

The famous sculpture of Abraham Lincoln in the Lincoln Memorial was designed by Daniel Chester French and carved by the Piccirilli Brothers of New York. The Lincoln Memorial, modeled after the Parthenon in Athens, was dedicated on May 30, 1922.

generation of writers. Talented young authors, coming to terms with the brutality and failed promises of "the war to end all wars," as World War I was called, imbued their writing with a sense of disillusionment and alienation. There was a spirit of rebellion, a desire to break from the past and view the world in a cold, harsh light. Victorian ideas of decency were derided as hypocritical, and many young writers dealt frankly with sexuality. They fought against the censorship of profanity and incorporated Freudian ideas into their characters and styles. The United States was perceived to be spiritually impoverished, a theme expressed in T.S. Eliot's most famous poem, "The Waste Land," written in 1922. To many, the probusiness, anything-for-a-buck mentality that ran rampant during

F. Scott Fitzgerald (1896-1940) and Zelda Fitzgerald (1900-1948)

F. Scott Fitzgerald is credited with coining the term "The Jazz Age," and together with his wife, Zelda, they were, for a time, its idols. Scott first met Zelda during World War I when he was stationed in Montgomery, Alabama, her home town. The eighteen-year-old Zelda was so beautiful and popular that young army pilots regularly flew stunts over her home until the commanding officer forbade it. Though Zelda and Scott quickly fell in love, she hesitated to marry him because he had not yet proven to be a money-maker.

That all changed with the publication of Scott's first novel, *This Side of Paradise*, in 1920. The story of a young Princeton undergraduate unlucky in love, the book was unpolished and weak in spots, but it also marked the arrival of an exciting, original voice, the voice of impatient youth. In it, Scott gave accurate, nonjudgmental descriptions of petting parties and flirtatious flappers that shocked much of the public. Most disturbing to some was his portrayal of postwar disillusionment among the young: "Here was a new generation...grown up to find all Gods dead, all wars fought, all faiths in man shaken."

With his newfound fame and fortune, Scott won Zelda's hand in marriage, and the two of them became the toast of New York. They hopped from party to party, drinking bootleg liquor, diving into fountains, and dancing on tabletops. With their beauty, their wittiness, and their wild antics, they seemed to personify the youthful ideal of the Roaring Twenties. In the process, they also ran up incredible tabs, though Scott always seemed to be shocked to find they were in debt. To pay for their extravagant lifestyle, Scott wrote prolifically, mostly for slick magazines. Much of what he wrote was not up to his level of talent, and at times, he became disgusted with himself for letting the high life get in the way of his serious work.

Scott and Zelda Fitzgerald, with daughter Scottie.

He wrote to his editor that he wanted to create " ... something extraordinary and beautiful and simple and intricately patterned." With the publication of *The Great Gatsby* in 1925, he succeeded. Though the novel is widely considered his best work, it did not sell well when it first appeared.

Meanwhile, Scott was slipping further and further into alcoholism. His and Zelda's never ending quest for excitement grew increasingly desperate, and their attempts to shock others was alienating their friends. Fellow writer John Dos Passos remembered their behavior at an elegant outdoor dinner party in the French Riviera: "Scott and Zelda got drunk on the cocktails and instead of coming to the table crawled among the vegetables on all fours tossing an occasional tomato at the guests."

While Scott's drinking problem escalated, Zelda also grew unstable. A talented amateur writer and painter, Zelda was jealous of Scott's success. At the age of twenty-seven, she began to seriously study ballet, and though she practiced until her legs were bruised and her feet bled, she had started much too late in life to achieve success as a ballerina. That realization led to a nervous breakdown, and she spent the rest of her life in and out of asylums.

A character in "One Trip Abroad," a story Scott wrote in 1929, seems to sum up his state of mind as the Jazz Age drew to a close: "It's just that we don't understand what's the matter. Why did we lose peace and love and health, one after the other?"

CULTURE AND SOCIETY

For further information see primary source entries on pages

11: 1469-70, 1509-10, 1516-18, 1520;
12: 1613-17, 1671-73, 1719-21

Ernest Hemingway spent most of the twenties living and writing in Paris. His first literary success came with The Sun Also Rises, *published in 1926.*

Coolidge Prosperity was symptomatic of the moral emptiness of the United States. They also despaired that standardization was weakening American culture, making it bland and dull.

In the United States, the exciting center of the literary world was Greenwich Village in New York City, which already had a reputation as a magnet for radicals. But those who sought to escape the dullness and hypocrisy of the United States went to Europe, especially to Paris, where there was a thriving community of expatriates. Many of them gathered at the well-known salon of American writer Gertrude Stein, who is credited with referring to these young writers and artists as a "lost generation." In a 1927 interview, F. Scott Fitzgerald explained, "The best of America drifts to Paris. The American in Paris is the best American. It is more fun for an intelligent person to live in an intelligent country." It is also a pleasure to get more for your money, and in the twenties, the dollar was very strong in France, an important consideration to a struggling young writer. Another benefit was that, without the restraints of prohibition, wine flowed freely in Paris.

From this group of expatriates a young writer emerged who would have a tremendous impact on American

literature. Ernest Hemingway joined World War I as a volunteer ambulance driver in France and later entered the Italian army. He stayed in Paris for most of the decade writing short stories, poems, and novels, though for a time his work only excited interest among his literary colleagues. From Hemingway's perspective, the world was senseless and often cruel, and the best an individual could do was to face it stoically, with courage. His style exhibits that philosophy with terse, simple sentences and a dispassionate tone. His was a fresh, new voice, and

Puritanism: "The haunting fear that someone, somewhere, may be happy."

H.L. Mencken

H. L. Mencken. (1880-1956)

Journalist, editor, social critic, and political commentator, Henry Louis Mencken was one of the most controversial and influential figures of the twenties. He came to be known as the "Sage of Baltimore," where he was born and lived throughout his life. One of Mencken's literary heroes was Mark Twain. Like Twain, he viewed the human animal as a flawed creature and used laughter as a weapon.

Armed with a sharp wit, Mencken was quick to attack pretensions wherever he perceived them. He mocked sentimentality and delighted in getting a rise out of his readers. At times, it seemed that Mencken was against anything that mainstream Americans were for, including democracy and religion. He had no faith in the middle class, which he referred to as the "booboisie."

Mencken's positions against all authority and conventions made him a hero to the rebellious "Young Intellectuals" of the twenties. In 1924, he and George Nathan launched a magazine called *American Mercury*, which sought to explore, as Mencken put it, "the whole gaudy, gorgeous American scene." Its audience was mainly college students, Greenwich Village bohemians, and people who considered themselves, or wished others to consider them, freethinkers. Mencken actively sought out talented young writers and gave them a forum in his magazine. F. Scott Fitzgerald once wrote to the Sage that Mencken's opinion of his book was more important to him than anyone else's. Mencken was cynical of democracy and racial equality and is now considered antisemitic because of his racist outpourings.

In 1926, the April issue of *American Mercury* was banned in Boston for an article about a small-town prostitute. It was just the type of free speech fight that Mencken loved. In a prearranged event, Mencken was arrested for selling the magazine to the reverend who orchestrated the ban. A judge decided that the article was not obscene and Mencken was acquitted, but critics accused him of pulling a publicity stunt.

Mencken's angry rebelliousness struck a chord in the twenties, but in the anxious, trying years of the Depression, the Sage's influence waned and his popularity faded.

H. L. Mencken is shown here selling issues of his banned American Mercury *magazine in 1926.*

Edna St. Vincent Millay. (1892-1950)

In the early twenties, poet Edna St. Vincent Millay was perhaps the biggest celebrity of the bohemian Greenwich Village set. Her poems expressed her disdain for the conventional, secure life and her desire to live for the moment, drinking in all the beauty and sadness that the world offered. She was young, beautiful, witty, and eloquent, a vivid example of the liberated woman. She believed in free love with a carefree, sometimes even flippant attitude, expressed in these lines: "And if I loved you Wednesday, / Well, what is that to you? / I do not love you Thursday / So much is true."

But if all of her poems had such a frivolous tone, Edna Millay would not be the enduring figure in American literature that she remains. In later poems, she contemplates why love fades away and explores the struggle to give oneself completely to love without losing one's identity. In 1923, Edna Millay won the Pulitzer Prize for Poetry. Two years later, she moved with her husband to a farmhouse in upstate New York.

As a poet, Millay continued to mature. In 1928, she published a collection of poems entitled *The Buck in the Snow*. The poem, "Moriturus," included in the collection, begins: "If I could have / Two things in one: / The peace of the grave, / And the light of the sun; ... " This was a recurring theme in Millay's poems — the inevitability of death and the peace that it offers versus the burning desire to live life in all of its beauty and pain.

In some ways, Edna Millay was a bridge between nineteenth century and modern poetry. Though she employed traditional rhyme schemes and meters, she used them to express modern, unconventional perspectives. And though she sprinkled her poems with "O's" and "thoust's," she also created fresh, exciting imagery and a sense of spontaneity.

uniquely American. Hemingway achieved his first popular success with the 1926 novel, *The Sun Also Rises*, about a disillusioned group of expatriates in Europe, followed by *A Farewell to Arms* in 1929. They were just the first two of a number of classics Hemingway would contribute to American literature.

F. Scott Fitzgerald is another writer who arrived on the literary scene in the twenties, giving voice to the confusion and disappointment of the postwar generation. Many of his stories and novels bring to life the wild, giddy, party atmosphere of the twenties, and for that reason, his name is inextricably tied to the "Jazz Age." But his best work also conveys deep, lasting themes, as in *The Great Gatsby*, wherein he portrays the American Dream, the belief that, through hard work, anyone can achieve almost anything, as an unattainable myth.

One of the most popular writers during the twenties was Sinclair Lewis. In 1920, he created a sensation with his novel, *Main Street*, a satirical look at small town life. His next novel, *Babbitt*, published two years later, sold even more copies and caused an even greater stir. This time, the target of Lewis's satire was the average American businessman, in the form of George

Babbitt, a realtor in the fictional town of Zenith. George is a model citizen, a town booster, member of the Elks, and eager to be accepted by the "right" circles of society. The conflict and the humor of the novel arise when George has something of a midlife crisis and begins experimenting with an unconventional life. In 1926, Lewis was awarded the Pulitzer Prize for his novel *Arrowsmith*. He shocked the nation by declining to accept the award because, he explained, such prizes were dangerous, and he did not want to contribute to the power they exerted over writers.

The satirical view of mainstream American life that Lewis conveyed in his novels was given an even sharper edge by H. L. Mencken, the most influential social commentator of the time. Mencken sought to deflate the pompous, expose the hypocritical, and ridicule the ignorant. He took on religious leaders, patriots, and even democracy itself. Sometimes Mencken chose vulnerable, obvious targets and attacked them with a viciousness that won him many enemies. But his witty, irreverent commentaries were very much in vogue with those who liked to consider themselves part of the Lost Generation.

Plenty of other talents emerged on the literary scene during the twenties. Writer e.e cummings experimented with language and the established rules of literary genre in poems, plays, and novels. Poet Edna St. Vincent Millay expressed the defiance and desires of her generation in simple, clear, direct verse. William Faulkner was an important part of what came to be known as the Southern Renaissance in literature. He won critical acclaim in 1929 with *The Sound and the Fury*, an unconventionally organized novel that takes a dark look at the downfall of a southern family.

It was an exciting period in American literature. Though most of this new generation of writers were critical of their country, they played a huge role in advancing the image of American literature.

The Emerging American Identity

Innovations were also taking place in American drama, art, architecture, and music during the twenties. Though the theater was still dominated by the melodrama and glitz of Broadway, young playwrights and stage designers were rejecting the old formulas in favor of a new realism and experimental methods. In plays such as Maxwell Anderson's *What Price Glory?* they presented realistic descriptions of the war, including profane language. Battles with the censors were common. But the writer who did the most to draw the world's attention to American drama was Eugene O'Neill. As a playwright and director, O'Neill boldly experimented with sets, characterization, and the form of the play. From a uniquely modern and American perspective, he presented a tragic view of life.

In the art world, American painters were producing exciting results from their interpretations of the modern landscapes and cityscapes that surrounded them. Edward Hopper portrayed the ever-expanding cities as cold, lonely, and alienating. Charles Sheeler earned his living as a photographer, and the influence of that medium is strongly felt in his sharp, realistic depictions of city streets and machines. He stripped away details until hard, geometric

Eugene O'Neill. (1888-1953)

Working with an avant garde theater group called the Provincetown Players, Eugene O'Neill began writing experimental, one-act plays before World War I. By 1920, he had gained a reputation as an innovative playwright and director. A prolific writer, O'Neill used his plays to delve deeply into the moral dilemmas facing modern men and women and presented humankind as inevitably flawed and tragic.

The Emperor Jones, produced in 1920, was one of O'Neill's first popular plays. In it, a former Pullman porter on the run from a murder charge has become a dictator of a West Indies island. The action of the play consists mainly of his attempt to escape a band of rebels on the island who are trying to kill him. O'Neill accurately depicts the progression of panic in the character's mind through his monologue and a steady drum beat, which gradually grows faster and faster, echoing his heartbeat.

O'Neill was greatly influenced by Freudian ideas and the attempts of psychology to unfold the mysteries of the human mind. In an attempt to dissect the psyches of his characters, O'Neill sometimes used masks. He also made extensive use of a device called the "aside," by which the characters speak their thoughts directly to the audience. Like many writers in the twenties, O'Neill attacked hypocritical puritanism, but he also explored the tragic loss of religion and its effects. In *Dynamo*, produced in 1929, he tells the highly symbolic story of a young man who rejects religion and comes to worship science instead. It ends in tragedy.

O'Neill was consistently ambitious in the subjects he chose and in the methods he used to convey them. Sometimes the effects were powerful; other times his drama seemed repetitious and heavy handed. In *Strange Interlude*, produced in 1928, he offered an in-depth profile of a modern woman, spanning thirty years in her life. The play consisted of nine acts and was five and a half hours long (minus an eighty minute intermission). It was a monumental, innovative effort, and though the play had its faults, where it succeeded, it was brilliant.

shapes came through. Georgia O'Keeffe produced beautiful, romantic paintings of skyscrapers, though she is more known for her depictions of bleached cow skulls and the barren, southwestern landscape. She also painted flowers from such an extreme close-up perspective that they became abstracted. Unlike most artists of the day, O'Keeffe did not receive any training in Europe, and her paintings represent an original, American vision.

It took only one glance at the cityscapes of New York and Chicago to see what direction architecture was taking — up towards the sky. In the second half of the decade especially, skyscrapers were being constructed at an incredible rate. Though critics complained about the congestion that resulted from clusters of skyscrapers, there seemed to be no stopping the wave of the future. Still, architects often turned to elements of the past to adorn their buildings, including Greek or Gothic flourishes. In 1925, construction was completed on the Tribune Tower in Chicago. Though it reached skyscraper heights with thirty-four floors and a 450-foot tower, it also reached into the past with elaborate Gothic buttresses. On the other hand, Frank Lloyd Wright continued to design organic buildings that blended into the surrounding environment. He believed in beauty born of simplicity and designed buildings to be practical, making the best use of modern materials. In 1922, construction was completed on the Imperial Hotel in Tokyo, which Wright designed to be functional as well as beautiful, taking into consideration the area's history of earthquakes. In 1923, an earthquake practically levelled the city. Wright's Imperial Hotel was one of the few buildings left standing.

The Jazz Age

One of the most original and enduring American contributions to music came from African-Americans. Though jazz originated earlier, it became popular with white audiences in the twenties, and as a result, jazz not only swept the nation but was exported to other countries as well. Born from a combination of African and European rhythms, jazz came to life in New Orleans. As played by the early African-American and Creole musicians, jazz was mainly improvisational, and most of them neither read nor wrote music. As the innovative pianist Jelly Roll Morton explained, jazz was not what you played, but how you played it. The unconventional rhythms of jazz carry a spirit of exuberant rebellion that was just right for the twenties. The blues, which had been around as a musical form since before the turn of the century, also flourished at this time. Rooted in the work song format that slaves used to sing, the blues were dominated in the twenties by women singers, the most powerful and talented of whom was Bessie Smith. Though discovered by whites

The elaborate Gothic buttresses of the Tribune Tower in Chicago are depicted here on this 1925 poster by Norman Erickson.

George Gershwin composing at the piano. His most famous composition, "Rhapsody in Blue," produced in 1924, was the first piece of jazz music written for the concert hall.

only shortly before her death in 1937, she was beloved by millions of African-Americans during her heyday, from 1923 to 1928.

During and after the war, many jazz musicians joined the migration to northern industrial cities, and soon jazz could be heard in the nightclubs of Chicago and New York. Jazz greats such as Morton and Louis Armstrong began recording their music. With the help of the phonograph and radio, jazz attracted an ever-increasing white audience. Speakeasies were also a great venue for jazz, as its lively, hot rhythm

Louis Armstrong. (1898?-1971)

Although many people remember Louis Armstrong as the jovial jazz entertainer of his later years, his important role in music history stems from the vital contributions he made to the development of jazz in the twenties and early thirties. Born into poverty in New Orleans, Armstrong was sent to the Colored Waifs' Home in 1912 or 1913. It was there that he received his first formal training on the cornet. He went on to study with the premier New Orleans horn player Joe "King" Oliver, and it was Oliver who summoned Armstrong north to Chicago in 1922 to join his band.

From early on, Armstrong displayed a natural ability, innovative style, and emotional depth in his playing. Oliver's pianist and Armstrong's soon-to-be wife, Lil Hardin, per-

suaded the young horn player to leave the restrictive environment of King Oliver's Creole Jazz Band so that he could give his talent freer reign. In 1924, he accepted an offer to join Fletcher Henderson's big band in New York. He soon became a featured soloist and vocalist and attracted much attention, though he was still mainly known within musicians' circles.

His influence spread when he returned to Chicago and began recording with his own ensemble, The Hot Five, and later, The Hot Seven. Recordings such as "Cornet Chop Suey" and "West End Blues" show his creative mind and incredible talent at work. The records, along with regular performances at popular clubs such as The Sunset in Chicago, earned him a reputation as the world's greatest jazz trumpeter. Musicians came from all around to study his virtuoso technique and his daring improvisations. No matter how complex the arrangement he played, he filled out every note, fully shaped every phrase, and did it with an unhurried swing that set the standard for other musicians. His warm-hearted, husky vocals were popular and influential too, especially his scat singing, made up of nonsense syllables.

Though in later years, Armstrong took his career down a more commercial path, with a greater emphasis on showmanship than on innovation, during the twenties he took jazz to new heights, performing classic versions of songs such as "Body and Soul" that are unmatched to this day.

seemed to add to the excitement of sneaking past prohibition.

As white musicians began playing jazz, a different style emerged. It was less improvisational, smoother, and had a more regular melody, making it easier to dance to. Typical of the faddish times, a dance craze swept the country as young converts to jazz flocked to large halls to hear it played by big bands.

In 1924, jazz was taken to a new level by a young composer and pianist named George Gershwin. Accompanied by an orchestra, he performed *Rhapsody in Blue*, a piece combining elements of classical, jazz, and popular music. The result was a totally original sound. Though some traditional music lovers rejected jazz as crude, others loved it, including Sergei Koussevitzky, then conductor of the Boston Symphony. "Jazz has come to stay," he said, "because it is an expression of the times, of the breathless, energetic, superactive times in which we are living; it is useless to fight against it."

The Harlem Renaissance

While jazz was having a tremendous impact on American music, the African-American voice was making itself heard in the literary world. The voice came most loudly from Harlem. What began as an affluent white neighborhood of New York in the nineteenth century became the preeminent black enclave of the twenties when the real estate market went bust there. In a panic, property owners subdivided the lavish apartments and rented them to the African-Americans who were arriving from the South and the Caribbean. By 1925, Harlem was almost totally black. Just as in the south side of Chicago and other large black neighborhoods, Harlem suffered from overcrowding and the crushing combination of high rents and low pay for tenants.

But Harlem also attracted a population of black intellectuals, writers, and artists. It became known as the center of African-American culture. There was a surge of black pride and interest in African culture and history as an atmosphere of creativity and optimism developed. Young talents were advised and encouraged by older, more established blacks, including poet/novelist Charles Johnson, who edited the Urban League's journal *Opportunity*, and

White audiences flocked to hear the all-black jazz bands. One of the most popular played at the Cotton Club and was led by "Duke" Ellington, shown here (center).

Langston Hughes. (1902-1967)

Though he grew up in the Midwest, by age nineteen Langston Hughes was eager to experience the stimulating atmosphere of Harlem that he had heard so much about. He enrolled in Columbia University in 1921, mainly because of its proximity to Harlem. He soon became so absorbed in the Harlem scene that he left Columbia and took odd jobs such as waiter and office boy to support himself while he wrote poetry. His poems expressed a pride in the heritage of his race and hope for the future.

In 1923, frustrated by his menial job and eager to see the world, Hughes became a mess boy on a freighter bound for West Africa. He threw all of his books overboard because he was afraid that he was beginning to rely more on them than on real experience to learn about life. For the next year and a half, he travelled through Europe and Africa, exploring the art and cultures of the countries he encountered.

After returning to the United States, Hughes's literary career flourished. He was awarded first prize for poetry in a literary contest and was publicly supported by one of the best-known American poets of the day, Vachel Lindsay.

Langston Hughes in his early days, when he worked as a waiter.

Many of Hughes's poems were inspired by his observations of the common people he met on the streets of Harlem. He wrote about the elevator man, the boy who cleans out the spittoons, the prostitute. Contrary to upper-class blacks, who believed that such depictions were degrading to the race, Hughes found inspiration in the urban blacks who faced hardship with humor and a strong will. He incorporated blues phrasing and the rhythms of jazz in his poems, shown in these lines from "The Weary Blues:" "Droning a drowsy syncopated tune, / Rocking back and forth to a mellow croon, / I hear a Negro play. Down on Lenox Avenue the other night / By the pale dull pallor of an old gas light ..." Hughes not only wrote poetry but also essays, fiction, and criticism. His accomplishments made him one of the most important African-Americans in American literature.

Alain Locke, a Rhodes Scholar, who edited a collection of essays, poems, stories, and illustrations by blacks called *The New Negro*. Some of the best literature to emerge from the Harlem Renaissance, which lasted until 1930, includes the poetry of Langston Hughes, novelist Claude McCay's *Home to Harlem* (1926), and Jean Toomer's collection of rural sketches called *Cane*. These works portrayed African-Americans as they actually lived, conveying their joy, their sorrow, and their daily struggles against a prejudiced society.

It was mainly the music of Harlem that drew white, middle-class New Yorkers to Harlem. Lavish nightclubs such as the Cotton Club featured the best of black jazz musicians, including the brilliant composer and conductor "Duke" Ellington and his band. Many of the clubs entertained only white audiences and were owned by whites, who were often gangsters, but other, smaller cabarets were integrated. By 1926, black entertainment became popular, and white audiences couldn't get enough of it. The Harlem Renaissance was no fad of the twenties; it had a lasting impact on American culture.

CULTURE AND SOCIETY

For further information see primary source entries on pages

11: 1469-70, 1509-10, 1516-18, 1520;
12: 1613-17, 1671-73, 1719-21

CHAPTER 9
The Problems with Prohibition

The Noble Experiment

Although President Hoover referred to prohibition as a noble experiment, it might also be called a naive experiment. No matter how honorable the prohibitionists' motives may have been, their goal, stopping alcohol consumption in a country the size of the United States, with a population of over one hundred million, was unrealistic from the start. Why, then, did the country go along with it?

The 1919 passage of the Eighteenth Amendment was the result of over five decades of effort by the Anti-Saloon League and the Women's Christian Temperance Union. The prohibition movement was supported primarily by evangelical Protestants, Baptists, and Methodists. In many ways, it was an attempt by rural Americans to stop what they felt was the corrupting influence of the growing cities. In the reform-minded prewar years, prohibition gained political support, due in large part to the intense lobbying efforts of the well-organized prohibitionists. Though "wets" and "drys" debated whether or not it was possible to legislate morality, the drinking

A "wet" parade in Washington D.C. in June 1919. Not everyone was delighted by the prospect of the coming prohibition.

public was generally apathetic. Some believed that perhaps their lives would improve if they were forced to give up drinking altogether.

But the nation was by no means unified behind prohibition. Though enough states ratified the amendment to make it part of the Constitution, some states did not sign on, and in those parts of the country especially, federal agents had a difficult time enforcing prohibition. More importantly, it was obvious from the start that many otherwise upstanding citizens were willing to flout the law.

Prohibition got off to an ominous start. During the 1920 New Year's celebration, over one hundred people were killed from drinking wood alcohol, a highly toxic alcohol made for industrial uses.

Bypassing the Law

On January 16, 1920, national prohibition took effect. Those who still wanted to imbibe, which was

A "moonshine" still in Kentucky, 1919. In the Appalachian Mountains, illicit stills had been in operation for many years before prohibition, but during the twenties, they multiplied and thrived.

PROHIBITION

For further information see primary source entries on pages

11: 1488-89, 1522-23

"I believe there is more bad whiskey consumed today than there was good whiskey before prohibition."

H.L. Mencken

a large portion of the population, were already looking for ways around the law. For the wealthy, it was fairly easy — they bought up as much wine, beer, and spirits as they could while it was still legal and stored it in their cellars in preparation for the dry spell. Those who didn't have access to such funds had to be a bit more creative.

Under prohibition, the manufacture of industrial alcohol for use in such products as paint was still legal, but it had to be denatured, or made undrinkable by the use of additives. During the early years of prohibition, diverted industrial alcohol was one of the major sources of illegal liquor. Bootleggers attempted to recover drinkable alcohol by removing the additives; they then added coloring and flavorings and sold it as gin or whiskey. The danger was that, in an attempt to cut corners or speed up the process, the additives would not all be removed, leaving the alcohol indigestible or even poisonous.

People also took advantage of other loopholes in the Eighteenth Amendment. Under the law, breweries were allowed to make beer, remove the alcohol content, and then sell it as "near beer." To replace the punch that the near beer had lost, speakeasy operators added grain alcohol, and the product was then known as "needled beer." One of the only segments of society allowed legal access to alcohol was doctors, who could prescribe it for medicinal purposes. Some doctors found it quite lucrative to write such prescriptions for their thirsty patients, though so-called "drugstore speakeasies" were not a major source of liquor.

As prohibition wore on, enterprising Americans became more adept at making their own beer, wine, and spirits. Illicit stills were already a part of life in the Appalachian Mountains, but during prohibition, those stills turned out more moonshine than ever before, with names such as "White Lightning" that hint at their potency. The process was cheap, quick, and easy to conceal in the rural countryside. Recipes for bathtub gin were also passed around, though most people actually mixed it in jugs rather than in their bathtubs.

Smugglers were the major suppliers of illegal alcohol, with two-thirds of their inventory coming from Canada. The long border between the United States and its neighbor to the north was impossible to seal, and bootleggers found it relatively easy to travel the back roads to pick up valuable Canadian whiskey. Until 1930, when the Canadian government began cracking down on smugglers, prohibition was a boon to that country's economy.

The other third of smuggled alcohol came from the sea. Large vessels sailed to the Bahamas, the West Indies, and other islands loaded up with cases of liquor, and then sailed to an area just outside of American territorial waters off the coasts of big cities such as New York and Boston. Stationed in "Rum Row," they sold their contraband to bootleggers who pulled up in speedy motor boats and then zoomed off, hoping to dodge the Coast Guard. While many bootleggers regularly passed off low quality liquor as premium brands with the use of false labels, a smuggler named Bill McCoy was known for selling only genuine

Scotch whiskey, imported from Nassau. His wares gave birth to the expression, "the real McCoy."

With so much bad liquor going around, access to a good, reliable bootlegger became a valuable asset and even a status symbol. When the wealthy wanted to drink socially, they could have quality liquor delivered to their homes to serve at cocktail parties. But most people could not afford such luxuries or safety. For the middle class and those seeking a little more excitement, there were speakeasies, usually tucked away in back rooms or basements of buildings. In 1929, there were an estimated thirty-two thousand speakeasies in New York City alone. The modest estimate for the entire country was 219,000. To gain entry, patrons had to make it past a guard stationed at the locked door who peered through a slot to check for recognizable faces or membership cards. The lure was not so much the expensive liquor and obviously not the mediocre food, but the atmosphere of forbidden fun. The famous speakeasy owner Tex Guinan was not far off when she greeted her customers with a call of "Hello, suckers!"

Nightclubs also flourished under prohibition. In addition to food and liquor, they offered entertainment, often including elaborate floor shows. Many nightclubs were run by gangsters who had enough influence that they didn't have to fear being raided. An evening at a nightclub could be quite expensive. On the other end of the economic scale, the working class drank at illegal saloons known as blind pigs. The alcohol served there was not only cheap but often dangerous, and those who imbibed risked blindness or even death.

Enforcing the Unpopular

To provide enforcement for the Eighteenth Amendment, Congress passed the Volstead Act, overturning President Wilson's veto of October 1919. The act made it illegal to manufacture, transport, or sell liquor. In a sign of Congress's ambivalence about the law, however, they did not make it a crime to buy alcohol.

Lobbyists for prohibition promised that enforcement would be cheap and effective. While the wets fervently hoped that it would not be effective, Congress counted on it being cheap. From the start, the Prohibition Bureau, the Treasury Department's agency created to ensure the enforcement of prohibition, was severely underfunded and understaffed. During the twenties, the entire country was covered by only fifteen hundred to twenty-three hundred agents and investigators. Until 1927, they received no special training and were not covered under civil service regulations. Though they often risked their lives confronting bootleggers and gangsters, the agents were seriously underpaid. As a result, the temptation to turn corrupt became too much for many of them. An average of one in twelve was dismissed for cause, and there were certainly many other crooked agents whose guilt couldn't be proved. The chief of the New York City Prohibition Squad reportedly summoned all of his agents, who legally earned only $2,000 per year, and ordered them to put both hands on the table. He then fired everyone wearing a diamond ring, which amounted to half the squad.

There were, however, some honest prohibition agents, and two of the most famous were Izzy Einstein and

"If you think this country ain't dry, you just watch 'em vote, and if you think this country ain't wet, you just watch 'em drink. . . . You see, when they vote, it's counted, but when they drink, it ain't."

Will Rogers

"Prohibition is an awful flop. We like it. It can't stop what it's meant to stop. We like it. It's left a trail of graft and slime, It don't prohibit worth a dime, It's filled our land with vice and crime, Nevertheless, we're for it."

Franklin P. Adams

Dodging prohibition was seen as a challenge by many Americans. Texas Guinan, shown here at her arrest in February 1927, owned one of the most successful speakeasies.

Eliot Ness. (1903-1957)

Though he attended the University of Chicago to study business and commerce, Eliot Ness longed to be a detective. After graduating in 1925, he worked for two years as a credit investigator, and, after learning the basics of detective work, became a prohibition agent. But Ness was quickly disillusioned when he discovered that the Prohibition Bureau was contaminated with graft. He was determined to break the grip of corruption and bring gangster Al Capone to justice.

Ness reasoned that Capone's operations could only be thwarted by a small group of honest agents who could be relied upon to not tip off the mob to their plans. Once he was given the go-ahead by the Department of Justice, he handpicked ten men to work with him.

The group was funded by the Secret Six, an organization of wealthy Chicago businessmen that had formed in an effort to put an end to the bombings and racketeering that plagued the city's business community. The Secret Six also helped fund the Treasury Department's investigations into Capone's tax evasion.

Ness's plan was to cripple Capone's brewing business, a major source of income, and by doing so, cut off their graft funds. Once the mob could no longer afford payoffs, they would lose their protection, Ness reasoned. His small group maintained the seal of secrecy and surprised Capone's gang with raid after raid. They seized almost fifty of Capone's beer trucks and destroyed millions of dollars worth of brewing and distilling equipment.

Capone's gang offered Ness and his men thousands of dollars in bribes, which were flatly refused. When the newspapers got wind of the story, they dubbed Ness's group "The Untouchables." Once he determined that he couldn't buy his way out of his troubles, Capone tried to have Ness killed. The young agent survived three assassination attempts, though his bodyguard was murdered.

In 1931, Ness's determination paid off. He put a handcuffed Capone on the Dixie Flyer and watched as the train departed for the Atlanta Federal Penitentiary.

Moe Smith. Not only did they make thousands of arrests, they gave the nation a few laughs as well. Einstein especially was known for his disguises. A short, chubby man in his forties, his tactic was to pose as an average Joe in search of a drink. Acting as a pickle salesman, for example, he offered a grocer reduced prices. When the grocer, in an attempt to return the favor, offered Einstein a low price on Scotch, Einstein nabbed him.

On the whole, however, the public's attitude toward prohibition agents was no laughing matter. The Bureau was given the unenviable task of enforcing a tremendously unpopular law, and when they did their duty by padlocking a speakeasy or shutting down a still, they were more likely to be criticized than praised. Still, they did seem to bring a

Famous prohibition agents Izzy Einstein and Moe Smith with a captured still. Not all agents earned the same reputation for honesty as these two.

portion of the public's loathing on themselves. The Bureau didn't win many supporters, for example, when they approved of treating industrial alcohol with poisonous additives, knowing that a portion of the alcohol would be consumed by drinkers. But what most enraged American citizens was when innocent victims were caught in the violence between agents and bootleggers. In ten years, 286 officers and citizens were killed at a ratio of one officer per three citizens.

Another problem with prohibition enforcement was that the judicial system could not keep up with it. Within a short time, federal courts were heavily backlogged with prohibition cases. In an attempt to avoid falling hopelessly behind, the courts instituted "bargain days," when large groups of defendants would plead guilty in exchange for small fines or short jail terms. Those cases that did make it to trial were more often than not heard by sympathetic juries, who were quite likely to decide for the defendant.

The Windfall for Organized Crime

One of the worst effects of prohibition was the power that it gave to gangsters. Organized crime existed before the twenties, but thanks to prohibition, it became hugely

Al Capone. (1899-1947)

Looking for help in running his Chicago crime syndicate, Johnny Torrio sent to New York in 1919 to hire a young gangster named Alphonse Capone. Capone came with a reputation for being ambitious and brutally effective, and in Chicago, his reputation grew. After Torrio was wounded in an assassination attempt, he emigrated to Italy, leaving Capone in charge.

From his fortified headquarters in Cicero, Capone set about consolidating his power by terrorizing the competition into submission. The Capone gang's killings were known for their attention to detail. After the rival Aiello gang let it be known that they would pay $50,000 for the assassination of Capone, the bodies of four potential hit men turned up around Cook County. Each of them had an unfired gun on his body and a nickel in his right hand.

By 1926, Capone was, as the newspapers called him, the "mayor of Crook County." Unlike other big gangsters who avoided reporters at all costs, Capone courted the press, passing around expensive cigars when they came to interview him and providing them with good quotes. For example:

"I make my money by supplying a public demand. If I break the law, my customers, who number hundreds of the best people in Chicago, are as guilty as I am. The only difference between us is that I sell and they buy. Everybody calls me a racketeer. I call myself a businessman. When I sell liquor, it's bootlegging. When my patrons serve it on a silver tray on Lake Shore Drive, it's hospitality."

Capone's cocky demeanor was due in large part to the fact that, in 1929 alone, his gang paid out an estimated $25 million in bribes. It put merely a dent in their $120 million income that year.

A believer in good public relations, Capone once paid the medical bills of a bystander injured in a shoot out and gave away five thousand Christmas turkeys to the unemployed. Still, a good deal of the press coverage he received was negative. He was, after all, a ruthless murderer and racketeer. And his regular appearances on the front pages made him impossible to ignore. President Hoover took a personal interest in putting Capone behind bars. Following a one-year sentence for carrying a concealed weapon, Capone was finally put away for eleven years in 1931 for tax evasion.

profitable. With money came strength and influence. As author of *Prohibition: The Era of Excess*, Andrew Sinclair put it, "In its practical effects, national prohibition transferred two billion dollars a year from the hands of brewers, distillers, and shareholders to the hands of murderers, crooks, and illiterates." These enormous sums of money enabled mobsters to buy the cooperation of police forces and politicians. Al Capone and Johnny Torrio, heads of the Chicago syndicate, used a combination of money and muscle to effectively take over the government of Cicero, a Chicago suburb, and run it as their own private kingdom.

Prior to prohibition, organized crime was primarily in the saloon and brothel business, and its clientele did not exactly consist of the most respectable members of society. But that soon changed. By providing quality liquor, the mob was fulfilling a public need, and the patronage of upstanding citizens raised organized crime to a new level. As for the violent nature of the gangsters' operations, the public was generally apathetic. After all, as long as they stuck to killing each other, who cared?

Still, the violence was hard to ignore. From 1924 to 1929, gang wars raged in Chicago and other big cities as mobsters fought over territory. The struggle between Capone's gang and that of George "Bugs" Moran for the north side in Chicago came to a head on February 14, 1929. Capone's men, disguised as police, lined up seven members of the Moran gang, who most likely believed that it was another routine raid. They were used to being searched. But this time, the "policemen" pulled out Thompson submachine guns, the weapon of choice among gangsters, and gunned the men down. No one was arrested for the crime. Though Chicagoans had grown used to gang violence, the St. Valentine's Day Massacre horrified them.

Automobiles were an important tool for gangsters, allowing for quick getaways. The supreme machine of gangster cars was undoubtedly Capone's custom-made Cadillac, featuring an armor-plated body, steel-encased gas tank, bullet-proof glass, and a handy compartment behind the rear seat for guns. It says something about General Motors' attitude toward the mob at the time that they were willing to build what was clearly the perfect gangstermobile for Capone.

With their flashy cars, dapper suits, and lavish funerals, gangsters were seen as glamorous figures by many, and some otherwise respectable people found it oddly fashionable to associate with members of the mob. But the public was also growing concerned with the crime wave. Violent crimes were increasingly carried out in the public eye, and the press splashed stories of gangland murders across front pages with sensational headlines. At the same time, the public's trust in those paid to uphold the law was waning, and for good reason. At the funeral of mobster Big Jim Colosimo, for example, the pallbearers included judges, congressmen, and aldermen. And of the 130 gang murders that occurred in Chicago between 1926 and 1927, not one resulted in legal punishment. It was clear that organized crime had permeated the political and judicial systems.

But the gangs' influence didn't stop there. It reached into the business sector as well. Gangsters already had experience in this field. For years, they had been offering their services to both capital and labor. Big business hired them to protect their plants and strike-breakers, and sometimes to "neutralize" union leaders. Labor had also turned to gangsters for muscle and protection. Empowered by prohibition, organized crime sought to profit even further through racketeering. Their procedure was to target a certain trade within their territory, and threaten to ruin the businesses of all

(Opposite) Notorious gangster Big Jim Colosimo and his girlfriend Dale Winter. Judges, congressmen, and aldermen were among the pallbearers at his funeral.

PROHIBITION

For further information see primary source entries on pages

11: 1488-89, 1522-23

of the members of that trade if they did not pay a regular bribe. In return, the gangsters promised protection from competitors who didn't cooperate. At one point in Chicago, there were at least sixty rackets, affecting everyone from milkmen to undertakers. The heavy cost of the bribes was, of course, passed on to the consumers.

The Prohibition Debate Rages

By the end of the decade, the debate between the wets and drys over the future of prohibition was louder than ever. Emotion was high on both sides, and the propaganda for and against flowed freely. The prohibition forces still had a number of strong supporters in Congress, and they were determined to maintain the amendment for which they had fought so long. The wets condemned prohibition as a violation of personal liberties and pointed to the past ten years as proof that it was unenforceable.

Though each side produced statistics to show that prohibition was either working or not working, the fact that most drinking occurred in private homes made accurate studies virtually impossible. The general opinion was that, while drinking had decreased especially among those who could not afford it, those who did drink were consuming more hard liquor than before. They were also drinking to the point of drunkenness more often. As Samuel G. Blythe explained in an article titled, "The Booze Complex," "No person can set out a bottle of booze now and hope to retain much of it for future dispen-

sation. It can't be done. 'Drink it all' is the motto; hurry down two, three, a dozen drinks for fear there may be no next time."

It was also clear that the working class was put most at risk by prohibition. Unable to afford quality alcohol, they were most likely to fall victim to amateur moonshine, improperly made home brew, or tainted industrial alcohol. An alarming number of people were blinded, crippled, and killed by bad booze.

Also disturbing to many was the blatant disregard for the law that surfaced during prohibition. To others, violating the Volstead Act was like striking a blow for independence, and wets wore their hip flasks like a badge of courage. As Blythe described it:

Here we see a vast public, from Maine to California and from Wisconsin to Texas, breaking the prohibition law on every occasion that offers and making the occasion when none offers; breaking it deliberately, joyously, continuously and expertly; breaking it methodically and not casually; breaking it openly and not secretly. Here they make a joke of it and have neither compunctions nor regrets.

When Herbert Hoover campaigned for president in 1928, he promised to set up a commission to investigate prohibition and decide its future. In 1929, he lived up to that promise, though the Wickersham Commission would not release its report (which included a confusing variety of viewpoints and did not support repeal) until 1931. In the meantime, Hoover pushed for stricter enforcement of the law. Within three years, the number of those jailed for liquor offenses more than doubled.

Hoover's hard line on violators did not necessarily mean that he believed in prohibition. He explained: "If a law is wrong, its rigid enforcement is the surest guaranty of its repeal. If it is right, its enforcement is the quickest method of compelling respect for it."

Hoover's statement proved to be prophetic, for with stricter enforcement, the dry law became more threatening to average citizens and aroused their protest. In 1929, Congress passed the so-called "Jones Five and Dime Law," which raised the maximum penalty for first time offenders to five years in prison and a $10,000 fine. Such severe measures motivated the anti-prohibition forces to organize their efforts and strengthen their fight for repeal. The Eighteenth Amendment was rescinded in 1933.

Society women flouting the law in a New York speakeasy, only too happy to try out the new drink – the cocktail.

CHAPTER 10
The Big Bull Market
and the Crash

The trading floor of the New York Stock Exchange during the 1920s.

"Everybody Ought to Be Rich"

By mid-decade, the recession of 1920-21 was only a memory for most, and business was taking in bigger and bigger profits and paying out larger and larger dividends. Plenty of people were looking to cash in on the boom, and the place to do it was the stock market.

Though some stock buyers held onto their shares as an investment, others played the market more actively, looking for quick gains. These were the people who gathered around the ticker tape machines, watching for daily market fluctuations and keeping their ears open for hot tips on what to buy next. They were encouraged by rumors about waiters, janitors, and maids who had earned small fortunes by acting on advice from their wealthy employers.

An increasing number of investors bought their shares on margin, meaning they put down only a portion of the value of the stocks (usually 30 to 50 percent) and borrowed the rest from their brokers. The stocks served as collateral, and the broker could sell them if the buyer was unable to repay the loan on demand. But as long as the price of stocks continued to climb higher and higher, that seemed like a slim risk to take, especially with such a likely payoff at stake.

With so many inexperienced stock market players eager to get rich quick, conditions were right for deceptive and unethical schemes to flourish, and so they did. One of the most underhanded methods was the speculation pool, wherein a group of investors would instigate a flurry of activity around a certain stock, sometimes even bribing financial journalists to write about the stock to create interest. Once they had driven up the price, they would sell out their shares, making a handsome profit. The price of the stock would then drop, much to the dismay of those who had followed the pool's lead.

Though not as blatantly corrupt as the pools, holding companies were also designed to reap large profits for the people who masterminded them. Primarily used by railroads and utilities, holding companies sold shares to the public while keeping enough shares to maintain a controlling interest. With the money raised by the sale of stock, the holding company would then buy a controlling interest in another company. Holding companies were often piled on top of each other, creating complex empires.

Investment trusts were based on a similar scheme. They were corporations that were formed to buy the stocks of other corporations. In other words, they did not create any

The economy boomed during the twenties and all America's industries were in overdrive.

"O hush thee, my babe, granny's bought some more shares. Daddy's gone to play with the bull and the bears. Mother's buying on tips and she simply can't lose. And baby shall have some expensive new shoes."

Anonymous

products or own any physical assets, but existed solely to provide stock portfolios for investors, and, of course, to make a large profit for the owners. Like holding companies, investment trusts were piled on each other, with trusts buying shares in other trusts.

For the first five years or so after the 1920-21 recession, the rise in stock prices seemed to make sense. Corporate earnings were up, and naturally stocks would go up too. But gradually, speculation on the Exchange seemed to take on a life of its own, independent of what was happening in the economy. Prices on so-called glamour stocks skyrocketed beyond all reason. For example, the Radio Company of America, or RCA, sold for $2.50 a share in 1921. By late 1927, it was selling for $85.00 a share, even though it had never paid a dividend. The big bull market was underway, and investors were eager to join in the frenzy and make their fortunes. Even *Ladies Home Journal*, appealing to the growing number of women speculators, published an article about stock market investing titled, "Everybody Ought to be Rich."

The Florida Land Rush

The stock market was not the only way to get rich quick in the twenties. In the previous decade, Florida's warm climate and improving transportation system lured a growing number of northerners down to the Sunshine State, where they bought property and built homes. As the area grew increasingly popular, land became more and more valuable, especially between Miami and Palm Beach. William Jennings Bryan, for

example, sold his modest home in 1920 and realized a profit of $250,000. He went on to lend his considerable talents as a speaker to a Florida land developer, extolling the virtues of the state's warm climate.

Soon potential investors were flocking to Florida by the bus, ship, and trainload. From the moment they crossed the state line, sometimes even before then, new prospects were pursued by aggressive salesmen, who wined and dined them and often provided free transportation all over the state to look at property for sale. Stories of success spread like wildfire, such as the tale of a man who traded his overcoat for ten worthless acres on the waterfront, which soon were valued at over $25,000.

The hard-sell tactics, combined with mouthwatering stories of overnight fortunes, were enough to wear down even the most cautious people. Journalist Gertrude Mathews Shelby traveled to Florida and reported that the frenzied atmosphere made people behave in strange ways, such as the young woman she met on a bus who exclaimed:

Florida? Wonderful! Came with a special party two weeks ago. Bought the third day. Invested everything. They guarantee I'll double by February. Madly absorbing place! My husband died three weeks ago. I nursed him over a year with cancer. Yet I've actually forgotten I ever had a husband. And I loved him, too, at that!

Investors often bought on the basis of blueprints alone, without ever looking at the actual property, which was quite possibly part of a swamp. For a down payment of 10 percent, buyers purchased a binder on the

A damp comment on the get-rich-quick schemes engendered by the Florida land boom, from Life, *November 1925.*

property, a legally binding written statement used until a contract is signed. Then they sat back and waited for the value to rise, hoping to resell the binder before the first payment was due. The same property was often resold four, five, even ten times within a year or two. The risk was that new prospects would stop flooding in.

By early 1926, speculation had raised real estate values to unrealistic levels in many areas, and the flow of newcomers was slowing down. There was a sense that the boom couldn't last forever. Still, investors rushed in to make their killing before it was too late.

The end came in the fall of 1926. Two hurricanes smashed into

Florida. The first, in September, killed 472 people, injured over six thousand others, and left tens of thousands homeless. Though not the only cause of the end of the boom (the real estate market was simply overheated and railroad lines to the state had become seriously overloaded), the hurricanes seemed to signify that it was time to get out. Miami and the surrounding area courageously began the painful process of rebuilding, but the boom had gone bust in Florida.

The Storm on the Horizon

A different kind of storm was brewing in the stock market, though many continued to forecast nothing but sunny skies. The fever of speculation continued to spread, and stock prices veered further and further from reality as 1927 turned into 1928. Economic indicators showed that industrial production was slowing down, business investment was tapering off, and unemployment was on the rise, yet stock prices rose an average of 20 percent in 1927. Speculators bought shares, not with a mind to invest in a solid corporation with a promising future, but as a gambler lays odds on a horse at the racetrack.

As the big bull market charged on, a few voices called out warnings, pointing not only to the unrealistic stock prices, but also to the corresponding rise in brokers' loans to clients. These were growing at an alarming rate, from one billion dollars in the early twenties to two and a half billion in early 1926, and then four billion in early 1928. Buying on margin was becoming increasingly popular,

and as speculators borrowed from brokers, they, in turn, borrowed from banks. But commercial banks were not the only available source. A high interest rate attracted money from foreign countries, much of it in the form of gold that was sent to Wall Street. American corporations also sought to get in on the lending game. Rather than reinvest their surplus funds back into their companies, many large businesses preferred to earn 12 percent on their money by lending it to investors.

Essentially, what made the stock market boom so precarious was that it was supported by speculators who fed on each other's enthusiasm, and if they began to bail out, a domino effect could send the market tumbling. The stock market's behavior in 1928 made the instability of the situation just about impossible to deny. In the early twenties, it was big news when two million shares were traded on the New York Stock Exchange, but that was nothing. In the spring of 1928, the frenzied activity on the Exchange broke record after record until June 12, when 5,052,790 shares changed hands as prices fell on many stocks. Still, speculators were undaunted, and in the next two months, the market recovered. It fluctuated wildly again after the election of Herbert Hoover, with average share prices rising 50 percent and then falling back down in December.

Despite this, President Coolidge told Congress in his last State of the Union address, in December 1928, "In the domestic field there is tranquility and contentment . . . and the highest record of years of prosperity . . . . The country can regard the present with satisfaction and anticipate the future with optimism." Speculators were more than happy to agree with Coolidge, and stock prices continued to climb in 1929. The average value of common stocks shot up from 117 points in December of 1928 to 225 in September of 1929.

There was a growing feeling among financial experts that the bubble of speculation needed to be deflated, but the delicate question was how to do so without causing an explosion. After taking office, Hoover met with leaders in the newspaper, banking, and financial fields, urging all of them to do what they could to discourage speculation, but it was to no avail. It would take nothing short of a disaster to stop the delirium on the stock market.

THE GREAT DEPRESSION

For further information see primary source entries on pages

11: 1529-35, 1540-50

ECONOMY

For further information see primary source entries on pages

11: 1526-28, 1537-39, 1550-53; **12:** 1611-12, 1680-81, 1702-03, 1722-26

Anxious investors wait for news outside the New York Stock Exchange on October 24, 1929. City police were called in to disperse the crowds.

The Crash

In the fall of 1929, the New York Stock Exchange was so active that it regularly saw four- and five-million-share days. Yale economist Irving Fisher optimistically predicted, "Stock prices have reached what looks like a permanently high plateau." But towards the middle of October, a downward trend in prices began to make people nervous. Newspapers reported that some brokers were asking speculators who had bought on margin to come up with more cash, because the value of their stocks had dropped to the point where they were no longer satisfactory as collateral for the loan that was used to buy them. Despite reassuring words from leading bankers, the feeling was simultaneously growing in thousands of speculators that it was time to bail out.

October 24, 1929, was destined to go down in history as Black Thursday. From the opening of the market, the rush to sell gathered steam, but many stockbrokers were unable to find buyers, much to their horror. Those who were buying were only willing to do so after the price of the stock had plummeted. Panic broke out on the floor. Word of the catastrophe spread quickly, and soon a crowd had gathered outside the Exchange. With the ticker tape running far behind trading, speculators across the country waited with dread to hear whether or not they'd been wiped out.

At noon, the news spread that a meeting of leading bankers was taking place at the offices of J.P. Morgan and Company, hosted by senior partner Thomas W. Lamont. When distressed speculators learned that the likes of Charles E. Mitchell, chairman of the board of the National Bank, were in attendance, they were somewhat calmed by the belief that a plan was in the works to alleviate the panic on the market. It was. After the meeting, Lamont met with the press to spread the word that the bankers were prepared to help. He calmly observed, "There has been a little distress selling on the Stock Exchange."

At 1:30 P.M., Richard Whitney, vice president of the Exchange and well-known floor trader for Morgan's,

These charts graphically display the rise and fall in stock prices before and after the 1929 stock market crash.

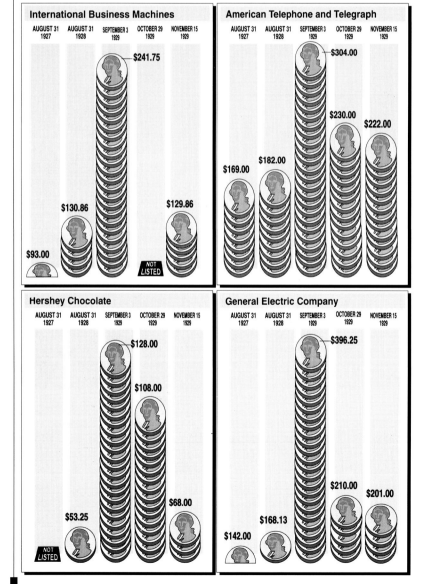

made his way through the crowd at the Exchange, attracting a great deal of attention as he did so. Then, using the money put up by the bankers who had convened earlier, he ordered ten thousand shares of U.S. Steel at 205, several points above the going rate. He went on to place fifteen or twenty more orders. The panic was halted, for the time being, at least. Prices made an amazing recovery, though most still closed lower than where they had started the day. On Black Thursday, an astonishing new record of 12,894,650 shares were traded.

Many believed that the worst was over, and financial leaders made positive statements to encourage that idea.

Eugene M. Stevens, president of the Continental Illinois Bank said, "There is nothing in the business situation to justify any nervousness." There was even talk of it being a good time to go bargain hunting on the stock market. But despite all of the pep talks, the worst was actually yet to come.

On Monday, October 28, the selling frenzy began again, with prices plunging to new lows. In the late afternoon, the bankers reconvened, but this time they concluded that the panic was beyond their control. On Tuesday, the situation worsened still further, with huge blocks of stock offered for whatever price they could get. But in many cases, no buyers

October 30, 1929. A New Yorker accepts his losses and bids farewell to the snappy roadster he bought when stock prices were rising. The car was quickly sold to a man who had kept away from Wall Street during the boom years.

stepped forward to take advantage of such bargains. Again the ticker lagged hours behind trading, and clerks were up all night recording the day's transactions. When it was over, a record-breaking 16,410,030 shares were traded that Tuesday. But more importantly, by now all of the gains of the previous year had been wiped out. Between September 1 and December 1, the value of stocks listed on the Exchange dropped by a staggering $26 billion.

Hoover and the Aftermath

Contrary to the popular myth, the stock market crash of 1929 did not lead to a wave of suicides. Though plenty of small investors and wealthy speculators alike were wiped out by the crash, most of them refrained from jumping out of windows. (Among the financial casualties was prizefighter Jack Dempsey, who lost $3 million in the crash.) Despite the great attention

The Great Wall Street Crash *(1929), by William Gropper.*

that the stock market attracted in the twenties, only a small portion of the American population was actually involved in it. In 1928, there were just three million shareholders, and less than half of their accounts were active. Nevertheless, the crash stunned the nation.

As the new president, Hoover did his best to calm the public. He stood by the statement he made after Black Thursday, that "the fundamental business of the country, that is production and distribution of commodities, is on a sound and prosperous basis." Many financial observers agreed with the president that the crash was caused by out-of-control speculation and not by any weakness in business or industry. Hoover was also not alone in believing that the crash was actually a healthy development because the market needed to be brought back to reality.

Though the crash hit early in Hoover's administration, there was reason to feel secure with him in charge, for he was no stranger to U.S. citizens. By 1929, Hoover had a reputation as an efficient administrator and a great humanitarian. A self-made millionaire, he earned his fortune as an engineer before turning to a life of public service. As the chairman of the American Relief Committee in London during World War I, he was hailed for getting thousands of stranded Americans out of Europe safely. He was also admired for his success in organizing food relief for Belgium and heading the Food Administration for the United States during the war. As secretary of commerce from 1921 to 1928, he pushed for standardization in industry and promoted commercial aviation, always looking toward the future.

Though Hoover believed that the crash mainly affected only reckless speculators, he realized that it might cause a slump in production and a rise in unemployment. Not one to sit idly by, he called together leaders in business and industry to urge them to maintain their payrolls and continue investing new money in their companies to keep business healthy. He also discouraged labor leaders from calling strikes to demand wage increases. For the government's part, Hoover pushed a tax cut through Congress, and spending on public works was increased at both the state and federal levels. Through these plans, Hoover hoped to prevent the sickness that had collapsed the stock market from spreading to the rest of the economy. But in truth, the economy was already ailing.

The Start of the Great Depression

What made the stock market crash inevitable was that speculators, who had been riding high on the wave of prosperity, didn't want to come down even though the tide was receding. The economic boom had been fueled largely by growth in two areas: the durable goods industries, including automobiles, and construction and real estate. But towards the end of the decade, the fuel began to run out.

As the phrase indicates, a durable good is a product that lasts a relatively long time, meaning that once the consumer has purchased it, he or she does not need to buy a new one for several years. By the late twenties, most households that could afford washing machines and other durable goods had already bought them, and

THE GREAT DEPRESSION

For further information see primary source entries on pages

11: 1529-35, 1540-50

Mr. Edward Thomas, a newspaper executive, and his wife enjoying a day at the races in Miami, Florida. During the 1920s, the gap between rich and poor widened. As a result, there was insufficient demand to keep up with the expanding industrial output.

the demand went down. Automobile sales had risen steadily all through the decade, but by the middle of 1929, that market too seemed to be saturated. During the second half of the year, car sales went into a steep decline.

The construction industry also flourished and then withered. After the recession of 1920-21 was over, construction went into overdrive to meet the demands caused by the postwar housing shortage. There was also a need for more factories, offices, schools, and roads to be built. The construction boom was a great boost to the economy. Conversely, when demand dropped and construction fell, the ripple was felt throughout the economy. So in 1928 and the first half of 1929, as speculators were pushing stock prices higher and higher, workers in factories, auto plants, and construction were being laid off. In other words, the stock market crash was not the only factor that lead the United States into the Great Depression of the thirties.

There were other precrash signs of illness in the economy as well. Agriculture was still in decline, with more and more farmers declaring bankruptcy and moving their families to cities. In factories, machines continued to replace workers, leading to the persistent problem of "technological unemployment." And though there is a general impression that incomes rose during the decade, in truth it was mainly the rich who were getting richer. The biggest increases went to those at the high end of the spectrum, and the number of people with salaries of $100,000 or more doubled between 1920 and 1928. Such maldistribution of income is often cited as an important cause of the Depression. Consumer buying power simply could not keep up with the increase in the number of goods being produced. In addition, foreign economies were facing problems of their own, which, combined with high tariffs, meant that international trade was decreasing.

On top of all of these other problems, as the twenties ended,

Americans were beginning to watch their pennies. The consumer society that advertisers pursued throughout the twenties had responded all too well. In seven years, the amount of personal debt in the country rose by 50 percent. Understandably, many Americans were feeling a bit nervous about this new burden of debt and decided to slow their spending until they could catch up. Unfortunately, they couldn't have picked a worse time to become frugal as far as the nation's economy was concerned.

With hindsight, the signals pointing to a weakening economy come into sharp focus, but in 1929, many were predicting a mild recession at worst. Even when the economic situation did not improve within a year as hoped, the atmosphere was still cautiously optimistic. Many refused to believe that the boom was over.

Autos parked on the sand at Revere Beach, Massachusetts, on a July 4 holiday in the early twenties. The auto market was saturated by the end of the decade and its declining growth hastened the general malaise in the economy.

CHAPTER 11
The Decade in Review

While America retreated into isolationism, disturbing events were unfolding in Europe. Hitler's Nazi Party was growing in strength and Mussolini's Fascists had marched on Rome. Here Hitler (center right) reviews a Nazi parade at Oldenburg, Germany, in 1930.

The United States in the twenties was an odd mixture of status quo and dynamic change, of conservatism and modernism. On the political and social policy scene, it was an uneventful decade, especially compared to the progressive years that preceded it. But from a social and cultural standpoint, it was a period of vitality, excitement, and upheaval. American society was going through some major changes, and though in some ways it was becoming more homogeneous than ever before, in other ways it was deeply divided.

Isolation and Republican Leadership

In the years following World War I, the United States demonstrated that, despite its newfound role as a leading world power, it was less than willing to take on the responsibilities that go with that status. The war had given Americans more than their fill of international affairs, and they eagerly returned to isolationism in the twenties. Though the decade began with President Woodrow Wilson pushing for U.S. membership in the League of Nations, which he created, Harding announced in his inaugural address, "We seek no part in directing the destinies of the world." The United States participated in League activities during the twenties, but refused to join it. It also declined membership in the World Court. Though tensions were building in Europe and a totalitarian threat loomed, the United States had no desire to get involved during the twenties. Washington's main concern regarding Europe seemed to be recouping its wartime loans. As President Coolidge said, "They hired the money, didn't they?"

On the domestic front, the Republican administrations of Harding, Coolidge, and Hoover all practiced a similar hands-off approach with regards to business. They operated on the philosophy that by giving big business the room to flourish, the rest of the country would prosper as well. The plan seemed to work, for many areas of business experienced tremendous growth during the decade, and most of the public agreed that business was the hope of the future. The pervading attitude was summed up in a 1921 article by Edward Earl Purinton entitled, "Big Ideas from Big Business":

What is the finest game? Business. The soundest science? Business. The truest art? Business. The fullest education? Business. The fairest opportunity? Business. The cleanest philanthropy? Business. The sanest religion? Business.

In other words, business held all the answers. There was no need for new social legislation.

Leaders of big business, for obvious reasons, saw a great deal of wisdom in the Republican policies, but others, including farmers, small business owners, and workers such as those in the Gastonia mill town, were not at all convinced that there was no further need for reforms. Still, they would have to wait until the next decade and the New Deal before their pleas for action would be heeded.

The First Modern Decade

Though bold initiatives were hard to come by in government policy, the social scene was an entirely different story. To the young moderns of the twenties, boldness was the ideal. But it wasn't just the flapers, their raccoon-coated boyfriends, and the Lost Generation who instigated a decade of change. Much larger forces were involved. Technology, science, urbanization, mass production, and mass consumption — all were changing the way Americans worked, played, and thought. As historian George E. Mowry explains, the twenties "prepared the way for the future."

While on the one hand, Americans sought to reap all the benefits that modernization had to offer, they were also afraid of what was being sacrificed for progress. As

Sheik with Sheba, *a drawing by John Held, Jr., from* Judge *magazine, 1925, sums up the changing face of twenties America.*

Geoffrey Perrett observes, "All across American life there was a deep break in continuity, with the sense of release that liberation brings, along with all the anxiety occasioned by the unknown."

Some people embraced the future, while others tried to hang on to the past. While the new generation rebelled against Victorian and Puritan ideas, modernism was a bad word in some circles. The revolu-

tion in morals and manners, especially with regard to the "new American woman" was considered a horrifying development by many. They pointed to the flapper as a sign of the coming downfall of civilization. And as sex and petting parties became more common topics of conversation, it was not only Victorian parents who began to worry about their daughters.

The booming cities were seen as hothouses of modernism, and as such they were disdained by rural, old-stock folks who held dearly to traditional values. As cities grew, so did the urban influence on American society, which was a threatening development to conservative people in small towns and the still-developing areas of the frontier. They associated big city life with free love, high divorce rates, "un-American" immigrants, and cynical, young nonbelievers. The Ku Klux Klan exploited this distrust and antipathy toward urbanization, and many citizens who wouldn't think of putting on a white sheet agreed with the Klan's leaders that what passed for urban sophistication was really moral decay.

Intellectuals were also considered a destructive force by many, for by promoting the theories of Freud and evolutionism, they were weakening the influence of religion. The rise of religious fundamentalism in the twenties was in part a reaction against the growing influence of science and psychology. While more people than ever before attended public schools and universities in the twenties, not everyone was pleased by this development. At a religious meeting in Dayton, Tennessee, location of the Scopes trial, preacher Joe

Leffew declared, "Some folks work their hands off 'n up 'n to the elbows to give their younguns education, and all they do is send their younguns to hell."

Technology and the Rise of Popular Culture

It was a confusing time for many, made more confusing by the speed with which new ideas, fads, and fashions spread from one end of the country to the other. One of the most important developments of the twenties was the "shrinking" of

(Below) Chicago in the twenties. To many conservatives the rapidly growing cities were seen as hotbeds of free love, high divorce rates, and immorality.

the country and the resulting effects on American culture. The automobile, radio, and movies all became extremely popular during the decade, and all served to make Americans less isolated from one another.

By the mid-twenties, a car was deemed so essential that, as the Lynds discovered while conducting their research for *Middletown*, some families who had no bathtub managed to buy an automobile. The auto enabled rural housewives to drive into town to visit friends, small town teenagers to drive to the movie theater, and vacationers to explore the country.

While the automobile brought Americans closer together physically, movies and radio bridged the gaps in other ways. With the proliferation of these two media, Americans all over the country from all walks of life were able to listen to the same songs and speeches, laugh at the same jokes, and admire the same fashions. As tabloids and magazines began reaching mass audiences, they too con-

An Essex Super Six of 1930. The automobile was the supreme status symbol of the twenties.

tributed to the rise of popular culture.

Advertising also took on a larger role in American society. With the twenties, mass-production came into full bloom, and it naturally relied on mass-consumption to keep the cycle going. It was the advertisers' job to keep consumers consuming by appealing to their tastes, desires, dreams, and fears. Movie studios, radio producers, tabloid publishers, and advertisers were all concerned with giving the public what it wanted. It was a trend that became increasingly important as the decade progressed.

Hero Worship and Charles Lindbergh

One of the results of the growing importance of the tastes of the crowd

Hero worship reached its zenith with the ticker tape parade in honor of transatlantic flyer Charles Lindbergh in 1927.

was that a rapid succession of heroes appeared on the national scene. Movie stars, athletes, and other popular figures were idolized by adoring fans who wanted to know everything possible about their personal lives, right down to their favorite foods. Publicity agents and tabloid journalists did all they could to feed this hunger for heroes, for they knew that it meant money in the bank.

But the biggest hero of the decade was neither a movie star nor a sports figure, and though he gained fame by participating in a hotel man's publicity stunt, he managed to rise above all the ballyhoo and appeal to a deep need in the American public. Charles Lindbergh came along at a time when grisly murders were detailed in tabloids, gangsters were being glamorized, and the debate over modern morals was as loud as ever. Against this backdrop, he flew his single-engine plane solo from New York to Paris. That alone would not have been enough to make him the most popular and famous man in the country. Mary B. Mullet explained, in the October, 1927 issue of the *American Magazine*, why the public reacted as it did to Lindbergh:

We shouted ourselves hoarse. Not because a man had flown across the Atlantic! Not even because he was an American! But because he was as clean in character as he was strong and fine in body; because he put 'ethics' above any desire for wealth; because he was as modest as he was courageous; and because — as we now know, beyond any shadow of doubt — these are the things which we honor most in life.

In short, Lindbergh combined the exciting promise of the future with the solid morals that many had feared were becoming a thing of the past.

The End of The Jazz Age

As a presidential candidate in 1928, Hoover had said: "We in America today are nearer to the final triumph over poverty than ever before in the history of any land . . . given a chance to go forward with the policies of the last eight years, we shall soon with the help of God be in sight of the day when poverty will be banished from the nation." In retrospect, with the benefit of the knowledge of what was to come in the next ten years, Hoover's words seem naively idealistic. But at the time that they were spoken, there was widespread optimism in the country.

Nicknamed the "Great Engineer," Hoover seemed to capture the mood of the people, many of whom believed that in engineering lay the answer to the country's problems. Technology had improved the average lifestyle, and though Coolidge Prosperity had not been evenly distributed, many benefited from it. The average work week dropped from sixty to forty-eight hours, and Charlie Chaplin was keeping everyone in stitches. But perhaps most importantly, when Hoover gave that speech, the big bull market was still climbing to new heights.

As president-elect, Hoover gave a much more prophetic prediction. On his way home from a goodwill trip to South America, he stopped in Miami to visit with friends.

Meditating on the responsibility that he was about to undertake, he said:

I have no dread of the ordinary work of the presidency. What I do fear is the exaggerated idea the people have conceived of me. They have a conviction that I am a sort of superman, that no problem is beyond my capacity. If some unprecedented calamity should come upon this nation I would be sacrificed to the unreasoning disappointment of a people who had expected too much.

It was the prediction of a very perceptive man, for to some extent, he too was the subject of hero worship. If anyone could keep Coolidge Prosperity going, it was Hoover, many believed. He had proven himself to be a great leader and a protector of the people by his reactions to such disasters as the Russian famine of 1922 and the Mississippi flood of 1927. But the calamity he was about to face was indeed unprecedented. As the twenties came to a close, the United States was on the brink of the Great Depression. Whether Americans wanted to believe it or not, the Jazz Age was over.

President and Mrs. Hoover in 1929. Hoover seemed to offer much, but was unable to extract the country from the economic morass of the Great Depression.

KEY DATES

1920

Business recession.

Sinclair Lewis's *Main Street* is published, as is F. Scott Fitzgerald's *This Side of Paradise*.

January 2 — At the height of the Red Scare, raids ordered by Attorney General A. Mitchell Palmer take place in thirty-three cities. Twenty-seven hundred people are taken into custody.

January 16 — The Volstead Act, allowing for enforcement of the Prohibition Amendment, goes into effect.

May 5 — Nicola Sacco and Bartolomeo Vanzetti are arrested for murder.

August 26 — The Nineteenth Amendment, granting women suffrage, takes effect.

October — KDKA in Pittsburgh becomes the first radio station to receive a government license.

November 2 — Republican Warren G. Harding is elected president; Calvin Coolidge, vice president. The losing Democratic candidate is James M. Cox; the vice presidential candidate is Franklin D. Roosevelt. Eugene V. Debs, imprisoned president of the Socialist Party, receives over 900,000 votes.

1921

Business recession.

May 19 — The first Quota Law limiting immigration is passed.

June 10 — The Budget Bureau is created within the Treasury Department.

August 9 — The Veterans Bureau is established.

September — Atlantic City holds its first beauty pageant.

October 18 — Peace treaties are ratified with Germany, Austria, and Hungary.

November 12 — The Washington Armament Conference opens. Secretary of State Charles Evans Hughes proposes sweeping cuts on future and existing naval ships.

1922

The World War Foreign Debt Commission is created to work out a realistic schedule of debt payments.

The Union of Soviet Socialist Republics is formed.

February — The first issue of *Reader's Digest* is published.

October — Mussolini and his fascist Black Shirts march on Rome, Italy, and seize power.

1923

Hitler is imprisoned after an unsuccessful attempt to seize power in the "Beer Hall Putsch."

The Mah Jong craze is at its peak.

January 11 — French and Belgian troops occupy the Ruhr in response to Germany's default on war reparation payments.

August 2 — President Harding dies in San Francisco while returning from an Alaskan trip. The stated cause is embolism.

August 3 — Calvin Coolidge takes the oath of office, becoming the thirtieth president.

1924

Congressional committees investigating corruption of the Harding administration reveal scandals involving the departments of Justice and Interior and the Veterans Bureau.

January 21 — The death of Lenin

results in a power struggle in the USSR.

May 26 — A second, more restrictive Quota Law on immigration is passed.

July — The Leopold-Loeb trial takes place in Chicago.

November 4 — Calvin Coolidge wins the presidential election, beating Democratic candidate John W. Davis. Charles G. Dawes is vice president.

1925

The Charleston dance craze sweeps the nation.

July 10-21 — The Scopes Trial takes place in Dayton, Tennessee.

October 28 — Colonel Billy Mitchell, an avid critic of U.S. aviation policy, is court-martialed for publicly accusing the military of incompetence and negligence.

November 21 — KKK Grand Dragon of the Indiana Realm David Stephenson is convicted of second degree murder in Indiana.

1926

Ernest Hemingway's *The Sun Also Rises* is published.

Hirohito becomes the emperor of Japan.

September 18 — A major hurricane smashes into the Miami region of Florida, finishing off the land boom there.

1927

Babe Ruth hits sixty home runs.

April — The image of Herbert Hoover is transmitted by television from Washington to New York.

May 21 — Charles Lindbergh completes the first solo flight across the Atlantic.

August 2 — Coolidge announces he will not seek re-election.

August 23 — Nicola Sacco and Bartolomeo Vanzetti are executed.

October 6 — *The Jazz Singer*, the first feature-length "talkie," premieres in New York.

December — Ford unveils the Model A.

1928

The McNary-Haugen Farm Relief Bill is defeated for the last time.

The United States is criticized at the Havana Conference for intervening in Latin American affairs.

August 27 — Fourteen nations sign the Kellogg-Briand Pact outlawing war. Sixty-two nations eventually sign.

November 6 — Republican Herbert Hoover defeats Democrat Al Smith in presidential election. Charles Curtis is the new vice president.

1929

William Faulkner's *The Sound and the Fury* is published.

February 14 — Al Capone's men carry out the St. Valentine's Day massacre in Chicago.

October 24 — Black Thursday. The stock market crashes. It plummets further on October 28 and 29 and continues to decline through November.

FOR FURTHER RESEARCH

Allen, Frederick Lewis. *Only Yesterday: An Informal History of the Nineteen Twenties.* New York: Harper & Row Publishers, Inc., 1931.

Altman, Linda Jacobs. *The Decade that Roared: America During Prohibition.* New York: 21st Century Books, 1997.

Boardman, Barrington. *Flappers, Bootleggers, "Typhoid Mary" & the Bomb: An Anecdotal History of the United States from 1923-1945.* New York: Harper & Row, Publishers, 1988.

Broer, Lawrence R. and John D. Walther Editors. *Dancing Fools and Weary Blues: The Great Escape of the Twenties.* Bowling Green, OH: Bowling Green State University Popular Press, 1990.

Candaele, Kerry. *Bound for Glory, 1910-1930: From the Great Migration to the Harlem Renaissance.* Broomall, PA: Chelsea House, 1996.

Chaplin, Charles. *My Autobiography.* New York: Simon and Schuster, 1964.

Chesley, Ellen. Women of Valor: *Margaret Sanger and the Birth Control Movement in America.* New York: Simon and Schuster, 1992.

Currie, Stephen. *We Have Marched Together: The Working Children's Crusade.* Minneapolis: Lerner, 1997.

Deutsch, Sarah Jane. *From Ballots to Breadlines: American Women 1920-1940 (The Young Oxford History of Women in the United States, Vol 8).* New York: Oxford University Press, 1994.

Epstein, Dan. *The Early Years to 1949: 20th Century Pop Culture.* Broomall, PA: Chelsea House, 2000.

Eyman, Scott. *Mary Pickford, America's Sweetheart.* New York: Donald L. Fine, 1990.

Freedman, Russell. *Kids at Work: Lewis Hine and the Crusade Against Child Labor.* New York: Clarion, 1994.

Green, Harvey. *The Uncertainty of Everyday Life, 1915-1945.* New York: Harper Collins, 1992.

Grossman, James R. *A Chance to Make Good, 1900-1929, Young Oxford History of African Americans.* New York: Oxford University Press, 1996.

Hakim, Joy. *War, Peace, and All That Jazz: 1918-1945.* New York: Oxford University Press, 1999.

Hanson, Erica. *The 1920s: A Cultural History of the United States.* San Diego, CA: Lucent, 1999.

Howes, Kelly King. *Harlem Renaissance.* Farmington, MI: UXL, 2000.

Isserman, Maurice. *Journey to Freedom: The African-American Great Migration.* New York: Facts on File, 1997.

Lindbergh, Charles A. *The Spirit of St. Louis.* New York: Charles Scribner's Sons, 1953.

Lippmann, Walter. *A Preface to Morals.* New York: The Macmillan Company, 1929.

McKissack, Patricia C. *Mary McLeod Bethune: A Great American Educator.* Chicago: Childrens Press, 1984.

Rich, Doris L. *Amelia Earhart: A Biography.* Washington D.C.: Smithsonian Institution Press, 1989.

Weinberg, Arthur, and Lila Weinberg. *Clarence Darrow: A Sentimental Rebel.* New York: G.P. Putnam's Sons, 1980.

Movies

The Mark of Zorro, United Artists/Douglas Fairbanks Pictures, 1920.

The Sheik, Famous Players-Lasky Corp./Paramount, 1921.

The Hunchback of Notre Dame, Universal Pictures, 1923.

The Gold Rush, Charles Chaplin Productions/United Artists, 1925.

Phantom of the Opera, Universal Studios, 1925.

The General, United Artists/Buster Keaton Productions, 1927.

The Jazz Singer, Warner Bros., 1927.

Contemporary Music

Rhapsody In Blue, George Gershwin, 1924.

Sweet Georgia Brown, Red Nichols, 1925.

Black Bottom Stomp, Jelly Roll Morton, 1926.

Button Up Your Overcoat, Helen Kane, 1929.

Contemporary Literature

Babbit, Sinclair Lewis, 1923.

The Great Gatsby, F. Scott Fitzgerald, 1925.

Color, Countee Cullen, 1925.

The Weary Blues, Langston Hughes, 1926.

The Sun Also Rises, Ernest Hemingway, 1926.

The Sound and the Fury, William Faulkner, 1929.

Websites

Comprehensive site for the 1920s
http://www.louisville.edu/~kprayb01/1920s .html

The culture and myths of the 1920s
http://home.earthlink.net/~timsamuel/home. htm

Harlem Renaissance
http://www.nku.edu/~diesmanj/harlem_intro .html

INDEX

Page numbers in *italic* indicate picture; page numbers in **bold** indicate biography

ACKNOWLEDGMENTS

The author and publishers wish to thank the following for permission to reproduce copyright material:

The Bettman Archive: 312, 318, 333, 336, 340, 342, 347, 357, 358, 362, 363, 373, 375, 380, 383, 390, 421, 422; Bettmann/Hulton: 369; Caufield and Shook Collection, Photographic Archives, University of Louisville: 353; Culver Pictures Inc: 328, 371, 417; The Granger Collection, New York: *frontispiece,* 297, 381, 409, 420; Historical Pictures Stock Montage: 301; Indiana State Library: 346; Peter Newark's American Pictures: 295, 302, 305, 319, 320, 327, 329, 339, 344, 355, 359, 364, 389, 391, 404, 407; Photographic Archives, University of Louisville: 335; Popperfoto Photographic Agency: 341; Reuters/Bettmann: 332; Springer/Bettmann Film Archive: 384; Topham Picture Source: 414; UPI/Bettmann: 294, 298, 300, 304, 306, 307, 309, 310, 313, 314, 316, 322, 325, 331, 334, 337, 349, 350, 351, 352, 354, 356, 360, 365, 366, 367, 368, 370, 372, 376, 377, 378, 382, 385, 386, 388, 392, 393, 394, 395, 398, 399, 400, 401, 402, 406, 411, 413, 416, 418, 423, 425.

The illustrations on pages 308, 311, 315, 330, and 412 are by Rafi Mohammed.

Page numbers in *italic* indicate picture; page numbers in **bold** indicate biography